Growing Up, Spiritually

Kenneth E. Hagin

Unless otherwise indicated, all Scripture quotations in this volume are from the *King James Version* of the Bible.

Fourteenth Printing 2001

ISBN 0-89276-504-6

In the U.S. write:
Kenneth Hagin Ministries
P.O. Box 50126
Tulsa, OK 74150-0126
1-888-28FAITH
www.rhema.org

In Canada write:
Kenneth Hagin Ministries
P.O. Box 335, Station D
Etobicoke (Toronto), Ontario
Canada, M9A 4X3

CONTENTS

PART IV

PART V

FOREWORD

Growing up is a process.

In this book we'll talk about growing up —
spiritually. Our lessons, which may even seem
unrelated, will be those that will help you to grow.

First, they will help you sum up your own case
to discern where you are spiritually. Then, after
you've located yourself, they will help you grow
out of that stage into another stage — *spiritually.*

PART I

Chapter 1

LOCATING YOURSELF

"...When he (Christ) ascended up on high, he led captivity captive, and gave gifts unto men...And he gave some, apostles; and some, prophets; and some, evangelists; and some, pastors and teachers; For the perfecting of the saints, for the work of the ministry, for the edifying of the body of Christ: Till we all come in the unity of the faith, and of the knowledge of the Son of God, unto a perfect man, unto the measure of the stature of the fulness of Christ: That we henceforth be no more children, tossed to and fro, and carried about with every wind of doctrine, by the

1

sleight of men, and cunning craftiness, whereby they lie in wait to deceive; But speaking the truth in love, may grow up into him in all things, which is the head, even Christ:"
                                        -Ephesians 4:8, 11-15

Evidently Paul didn't consider the church at Ephesus to be grown up yet. Did you notice he said, "But speaking the truth in love, *may grow up....*"?

And, "Till we all come in the unity of the faith, and of the knowledge of the Son of God, *unto a perfect man....*"

This is the King James translation. I think when it says "perfect" our minds tend to run off on a little tangent and we miss what he's saying to us. Moffat's translation reads, "until we reach maturity." The Amplified translation says, "that we might arrive at really mature manhood." Paul is talking about growing up to be a man, or a mature person, spiritually. "That we henceforth be no more children." He's talking about growing up spiritually, about reaching spiritual maturity, about becoming a full grown man spiritually.

God wants us to grow.

And the Bible teaches that there is a striking similarity between spiritual development and physical development. It speaks of at least three stages in spiritual development which correspond to three stages in physical development. They are:

2

babyhood, childhood, and manhood.

As we look at them in just that order and notice subdivisions under each one, you'll find that some of the characteristics true of each stage of natural development are also true of the corresponding spiritual stage.

And I believe somewhere we can locate ourselves.

Chapter 2

BABYHOOD

"As newborn babes, desire the sincere milk of the word, that ye may grow thereby:"
                                    -I Peter 2:2

Here in Peter the Bible speaks about Christians being "newborn babes." No one is born a full grown human naturally and physically. They are born babies, and then they grow up. Similarly no one is born a full grown Christian. You are born a spiritual babe, and then you grow up.

There's a whole sermon in just that fact. We are going to be held accountable for the spiritual babies born into the family of God around our altars and in our churches.

I pastored nearly twelve years and really you don't expect too much out of babies because they can't do too much for themselves. Someone else though can do something for them.

Too many times someone is saved on Sunday night and if they make a mistake before Wednesday night everyone in the church knows it, and is already fussing about it. They expect him to be living, by Wednesday night or the next Sunday, just as good a Christian life as they do when it took them years to get where they are.

A number of years ago I held a two-week meeting for a particular minister. We were scheduled to go longer but I cut it off.

Crowds were coming. The auditorium would seat 800 and it was comfortably full every night. People were responding. We weren't really having evangelistic services — I was doing a lot of teaching and praying for the sick — yet on Saturday night when I gave the invitation first for people to be saved, thirty-three adults came for salvation.

They stood across the front as I prayed with them and led them in a prayer. Then I sent them back to the prayer room where others would pray with them while I went on ministering to the sick.

The thing that so impressed me about this service was that of the thirty-three who came for salvation so many were young married couples who looked to be between the ages of twenty-five

6

to thirty-two. I learned later not one of the group had ever been a Christian; not one was a member of any church. I asked the pastor after the service about these young people.

He said, "None of the thirty-three were backsliders. They were all sinners who came to be saved."

That was unusual. I asked him if he knew any of them.

He said, "I don't know a one of them. They've never been to my church before."

I asked him, "Did you get their names and addresses?"

He said, "Oh brother, I just figure if they got anything they'll be back. You don't have to worry about them."

I said, "I'm closing the meeting tomorrow night."

People are born babies. They need to be seen about. They had never been to that church before. They had never heard any Full Gospel preaching before. They needed to be followed up and prayed with, talked to, and dealt with. They were newborn babies.

After a leading healing evangelist held a meeting in a certain city a pastor who had cooperated with it said to me, "I'm never going to cooperate with another one of those city-wide meetings. Never another one."

"Why?" I asked.

"I didn't get a person out of it," he said. "Not a one. Not a member. It didn't do me a bit of good in the world."

"It didn't?"

"No."

I asked him, "Did you get cards on any of the folks who came to the altar?"

"Oh yes," he said, "they gave me some cards. But none of them ever showed up."

I was talking to another pastor in the same town about the same meeting and he said, "We got twenty-nine new members out of that meeting. I wish he would come back."

"How did you get them?" I asked. "How did they happen to come to your church?"

He said, "Oh they didn't know anything about our church. I got the cards on some of them and visited them. I didn't just encourage them to come to our church, but I insisted they get in some good Full Gospel church and go on with God. And some of them came to ours."

We are responsible for babies. Babies don't know. Babies can't do for themselves. A newborn baby in the natural can't do much. He doesn't walk yet. He doesn't dress himself. In fact, he doesn't do anything for himself. About all he does is eat. And about all he eats is milk. Spiritually there are newborn babes. And if they get the sincere milk of the Word, they will grow thereby.

8

Innocence

The first thing that attracts you to a baby is its innocence. People say, "You sweet little innocent thing." No one thinks of a baby as having a past. It doesn't have one.

Do you know something? If you are a newborn babe in Christ, you don't have any past. You may have been as mean as the devil. You may have been the worst wretch that ever walked. But no matter how you may have lived, when you were born-again you became a new man in Christ Jesus and you don't have any past. God looks at you as an innocent babe.

II CORINTHIANS 5:17
17 Therefore if any man be in Christ, he is a new creature (creation): old things are passed away; behold, all things are become new.

Even though innocence belongs to the baby-hood stage of Christianity, it is one characteristic we should never outgrow. We should maintain this state of innocence for the simple reason that if we don't, we will fall under the condemnation of the devil and be defeated in spiritual life.

A new convert is simple, full of faith, ready and willing to learn. We should always maintain that teachable spirit. Yet sometimes when we grow older we sort of come to the place where we have a "know-it-all" attitude; a "You-can't-tell-me-anything" attitude. Those people no one can help, including God Himself.

A group of men gathered in back of the auditorium after service one night in one of the churches I pastored. As I walked up to shake hands with them one of the deacons said, "Brother Hagin, what do you think about..." and he mentioned a certain Bible subject. I found out later he did that purposely to bring me into their discussion.

"Well, I don't know just where your discussion is," I said, "and whether I could fit in or not."

The man the deacon really wanted to help spoke up immediately, "Well, I'll tell you. You or anyone else can't tell me a thing in the world about that Bible subject. I know all there is to be known on it. I know all about it."

I said, "If you do, you've got me beat. And if you do, you have every other preacher beat that I've ever seen or known of, or any other person."

He said, "Well, I know all about it. No one can tell me a thing about it."

But to tell the truth, that fellow was the biggest baby in the entire church. He didn't know all about it at all.

Keep an open spirit and a teachable spirit, as well as an innocent spirit, toward God and man.

10

Ignorance

Our two children are grown now with families of their own. In observing our babies and grand-babies I know this — a baby seems to think every-thing he can get his hands on is intended for his mouth.

A newborn puts his hands in his mouth. As he grows a little older and learns to crawl across the floor if he finds a screw it goes in his mouth, if he finds a spoon it goes in his mouth, if he finds a spider it goes in his mouth.

Babies are ignorant concerning these things. They don't know what should go in their mouths and what shouldn't. And babies have died as a result of not knowing that. They have gotten hold of something poisonous and it killed them.

In one case I know of, a 14 month old baby, crawling across the floor, picked up some spoiled food left there perhaps by an older child. Before they could get the baby to a doctor, it died. An au-topsy revealed the poisonous food. The parents went back home and found some of the food on the floor of a room which was seldom used. That little one didn't know he shouldn't eat it. He was ignorant concerning the effect it would have.

What am I getting to? The same thing is true

11

spiritually speaking. We need to be careful what goes into our spiritual mouths. We need to be as careful about what we read as we are about what we eat physically. Christians many times think nothing at all of gulping down some poisonous doctrine which will poison life spiritually, rob them of their spirituality, and ruin their testimony if they accept it.

A number of years ago a denominational minister was filled with the Holy Spirit and had a marvelous experience with God. I'll guarantee you this much, I know of no greater soul winner in any church than that man. He was outstanding. He would get people saved when no one else could. It seemed to me you could stand up the twelve best preachers in America and let all of them preach and give an altar call — then he could take the same crowd, preach to them, and get more souls saved than any of the others after they'd had first shot at it. That was his ministry; an evangelistic type ministry. But he got to reading after some false stuff, finally accepted some false doctrine, and got off on it. If he has won a soul in more than twenty years I don't know it and no one else does either.

I know of some born-again, Spirit-filled people who were soul winners, getting people saved and filled with the Holy Spirit. But they got taken up with certain doctrines. Some of them told me, "God is doing a different thing nowadays." No.

12

God's not doing a different thing nowadays. They're just off their rockers. He's still concerned about saving people. They just left the fundamental truths of the doctrine of the Word of God and went off on something that doesn't amount to a hill of beans.

Some things are actually poisonous in themselves. And some things it doesn't make a whole lot of difference how you believe on them — they are simply not essential to salvation and it wouldn't make any difference whether you believed it, or you didn't believe it.

But too many times Christian people will feed on everything in the world except the right thing, and will become poisoned. Then they lead disciples off after themselves. If the Spirit of God is in it, He is concerned about there being unity. Did you notice Ephesians 4:13 says, "Till we all come in the *unity* of the faith"? That which will divide Christians is not of the Spirit of God — it's of the devil. The Spirit of Love never divides.

I went into a Christian home once and saw some books I knew to be poisonous lying on a living room table. They were religious books, but they were poisonous. (We need not only be careful about secular books, but we need to be careful about reading religious books.) I purposely worked the conversation around to these books. I picked one up and said something about it.

This person was a born-again, Spirit-filled

13

Christian but they said "Oh that is the most marvelous book."

"Is it?" I said.

"Yes."

In the early days of my Christian experience I had happened to get hold of some of these books and had detected immediately the poison in them. So I just turned to certain pages and began to read certain things aloud.

"Well now, Brother Hagin, they give chapter and verse in there. I looked some of them up and those verses are in the Bible."

I said, "Certainly. If they didn't give some verses — though they may take them out of their setting — and a little Bible, folks wouldn't read it. If you were going to poison a dog he wouldn't eat just the poison. You have to put the poison on a good piece of meat."

Do you see what I'm talking about? You have to put the poison on a good piece of meat to get a dog to come. The devil will use some good scripture to get you to eat it, but he'll put a little poison on it. Be careful no matter who you read after. Don't read everything you can get your hands on. Unless you are a fully mature Christian and able to rightly divide it, it would be best not to read such things.

Years ago I held a meeting for a Full Gospel minister, a very well educated man, a doctor of divinity. Up to that time I had never seen a larger

14

personal library than his. There's no telling how many hundreds of volumes lined the walls from ceiling to floor. Being a bookworm myself I was interested in looking it over. I read some of his books while I was there in three weeks of meetings.

As we talked one day he said, "Brother Hagin, I'll be perfectly honest with you. There are some things I've read that I wish I'd never read. They bother me. They hinder me yet, though I don't read them anymore..." And he mentioned some of these books. They were religious books. But he said, "I just wish I had never read them. It hinders my faith today. It hinders me in believing God today."

It would have been better for him never to have built that into his inner consciousness. But he had.

When I start reading something that takes faith out of me instead of putting faith in me, I have enough sense to lay it down right then. Be careful what you feed upon. There is a saying used in the area of man's natural diet, "You are what you eat." The same thing is true spiritually, "You are what you read."

Irritability

Babies are easily spoiled. And when they become spoiled they become irritable. It's mighty

15

easy to spoil them to a light so that you have to keep a light on. It's mighty easy to spoil them to being handled and held. They are babies.

But the Bible says something about babies growing up. David said, "Surely I have behaved and quieted myself, as a child that is weaned of his mother: my soul is even as a weaned child" (Psalm 131:2). The Bible says concerning Isaac, "And the child grew, and was weaned: and Abraham made a great feast the same day that Isaac was weaned" (Genesis 21:8).

That ought to be a great day — that day when Christians grow enough to get off the bottle. But you know, it isn't. It ought to be a feast day; instead it's a cry day. I know, I pastored nearly twelve years. It's no wonder to me at all that we're not doing more in some of our churches than we are. If we do get a newborn babe in we don't have a bottle for it. Every bottle is in use. And the older babies are not going to give up their bottles. Every bed in the spiritual nursery is taken. And the older babies don't want to get up and give up their beds.

In the last church I pastored there were two ladies who lived next door to each other. Bless their hearts. They had been saved I don't know how long, baptized with the Holy Spirit and speaking with tongues. But that doesn't make you a full grown Christian. They were the biggest babies in the world. You'd have to run after them, and run after them, and run after them. They

16

wanted you to come and pet them. They would miss church Sunday for you to come over on Monday and pet them.

So I just quit.

When one of the deacons said something to me about it I said, "Brother, if you want to go over and visit them, you go. But I'm never going over there again. The longest day I live, or the longest day I pastor this church, I will never set foot inside their houses again. I'm tired of wasting my time with them. They are babies who want to stay babies. There are other people who can be helped. There are new people to be visited. And others are getting saved who can be taught."

You couldn't have taught those old babies anything. So I quit visiting them and never set foot inside their houses the eighteen months I continued to pastor that church. But do you know what? When they saw I wasn't coming again I believe they were more faithful to church than they'd ever been.

We ought to grow enough spiritually so that instead of someone's having to come and visit us, and pump us up, and prop us up, and pray with us, and feed us, we are able to be out helping others ourselves. When weaning time comes we ought to thank God for it.

Actually, if a child is weaned properly, when weaning time comes it will turn its face from the bottle. If it isn't, you have a cry on your hands. If

17

you can just keep people on the milk, they will grow. Peter said, "Desire the sincere milk of the word, *that ye may grow thereby.*"

I have actually had pastors say to me, in trying to tell me I was giving their congregation a little too much, "Now Brother Hagin, I know my congregation should be better than they are, but you have to be careful. All they can take is a little milk. All I ever feed them is a little milk."

I said, "No, you haven't even given them milk. You've been pastor here thirty years. If they had been getting milk they would have grown. Peter said that we would grow thereby."

They didn't grow; so they weren't even getting milk. They were just getting bluejohn. Bluejohn is milk with all the cream taken out.

Babies are easily frustrated, easily distracted, easily hurt. The Lord wants to bring us to the place where we're not so easily frustrated. He wants to bring us to the place where we're not so easily distracted. He wants to bring us to the place where we're not so easily hurt.

Chapter 3

CHILDHOOD

"That we henceforth be no more children...."
-Ephesians 4:14

Paul is talking about *spiritual* children here. He wrote this letter to the church at Ephesus and we know they had at least twelve men in that church. Acts 19:7 tells us about twelve men and I'm sure they had more. When Paul said "that we henceforth be no more children" he was talking about that they would be no longer spiritual children but would grow up spiritually.

Characteristics of the childhood stage of spiritual development are similar to the physical.

Unsteadiness

When my son was a boy of thirteen or fourteen, I told him to mow the yard. The way he grabbed that lawn mower and lit out you'd have thought he would have had it mowed in thirty minutes. Back then we had a push mower, the yard wasn't too big, and he could have had it mowed in forty-five if he'd kept at it. I had to go to town to attend to some business. When I came back after about an hour and a half, there sat the mower in the middle of the yard. He'd made about two strips after I'd left. I began to look for him. I asked my wife where he was.

"I don't know," she said. "Didn't he go with you?"

"No," I said. And I looked to see if I could find some boys playing ball on the corner. I knew if they were, that's where he would be. They were. And he was.

He was unsteady. You couldn't depend on him. As has been said many times, you can't put a grown head on a child. You can't. The same thing is true spiritually.

A mother tells her young daughter, "I want you to do the dishes and sweep the kitchen. I'm going next door for a little bit." The daughter starts out all right, but when the mother returns the dishes are unwashed or half done and she can't find Mary anywhere. She goes outside and begins to call her. After a while she goes to the neighbors on the other side and Mary is there playing dolls with Susie.

Children in the natural are unsteady ...unreliable...impressionable...spasmodic. Spiritual children are the same way.

When a new pastor comes to a church everyone comes. I've gone to pastor a church and people would gather around, pat me on the back, shake my hand, and say, "Brother Hagin, I want you to know I'm with you. I'm with you one hundred percent. I'm behind you." Six months went by and I didn't see them. Nine months went by and I didn't see them. I thought, "Well now they're behind me; they said they were." The trouble was they were so far behind me I never could reach them. They were too far behind to do any good.

Then as an evangelist I went from church to church holding meetings for several years. The first service or two some people would get right in and shake my hand and hug my neck and tell me, "Bless God, I'm with you. I believe this is it. We're going to have a meeting." Then we'd run two or three weeks without seeing them again. The last Sunday night when the pastor would announce we were closing I've had them run up to me, look at the pastor like he didn't know what was going

21

on and say, "He's not going to close this meeting, is he?" As far as they were concerned it had been closed all the time.

Curiosity

Children are full of curiosity. Just as sure as you'd come in with a sack and set it down on the kitchen table, our second granddaughter, about eight at the time, would be in that sack. She was full of curiosity. She wanted to know what was in there.

Some of these spiritual children that have never really grown up spiritually — though they've had time and opportunity — as sure as they can catch a little bit of gossip going want to know, "Who? Who?" They're full of curiosity.

Curiosity is the characteristic of a child. If you tell a child not to look in a closet, he is going to get in it as sure as the world. Curious. Spiritual children are the same way. They're always poking their noses in the other fellow's business. The Word of God teaches us to tend to our own business. God doesn't want you poking your nose into the other fellow's business. Learn to be quiet and tend to your own business.

I was pastoring a church when one fellow wanted to know what all I was doing with my money. I said, "What are you doing with yours?"

22

He said, "That isn't any of your business."

I said, "I don't consider it any of your business what I'm doing with mine."

He got the point. You know, it is no more the church member's business what the pastor is doing with his money than it is the pastor's business what the church member is doing with his.

Curiosity is a characteristic of a child.

Talkativeness

Children have never learned the value of silence. They are talkative. And you will find folks in the childhood stage of spiritual growth are nearly always talking.

Did you know the Word of God has something to say along this line? It tells us, "In the multitude of words there wanteth not sin...." (Proverbs 10:19). And, "...a fool's voice is known by multitude of words" (Ecclesiastes 5:3). We need to learn to be quiet. A child doesn't know any better so he's always blabbing.

I remember one time when my boy was three years old. We had gotten into bed late one Sunday night after church. I had preached twice and was tired. We all slept in one large room. He was in a bed across the room from us. The baby was in the crib. The lights out and it was dark.

"Daddy," he said.

23

I hadn't gone to sleep but I thought if I pretended to be asleep he would hush and go to sleep.

"Daddy."

I didn't say anything.

"Daddy."

I didn't say anything.

"Daddy."

I didn't say anything, and he just kept getting a little louder.

"Daddy."

Finally my wife nudged me and said quietly, "Why don't you answer that child?"

I whispered back, "Knowing him he'll get started talking." He was three years old and didn't know anything about the value of silence. He'd get started talking and you couldn't get him to shut up. I thought if I didn't answer him he would think I was asleep and shut up. But he just kept getting louder.

"Daddy. Daddy. Daddy."

Finally I said, "What is it, son?"

"What's tomorrow?"

I said, "Oh, be quiet and go to sleep. It's time to go to sleep."

"Well, what's tomorrow?"

"It's Monday. Now go to sleep."

"What's the next day?"

"It's Tuesday."

"Is tomorrow always Monday?"

"No, tomorrow is not always Monday. When

24

tomorrow gets here then tomorrow will be Tuesday."

"I thought you said it was Monday."

"Well, it was Monday, but when Monday gets here then tomorrow will be Tuesday."

"If tomorrow is Monday, how can it be Tuesday?"

"Well, that's just the way it is."

"What's the next day?"

"It's Wednesday."

"Will it ever be tomorrow?"

"Yes. Now hush and get to sleep."

"What's the next day?"

"Thursday."

"What's the next day?"

"Friday."

"What's the next day?"

"Saturday."

"What's the next day?"

"Sunday. That's today."

"Is Sunday always today?"

"No, it's just today today. When Monday gets here, it will be today."

"I thought you said it was tomorrow."

"Oh, now you have me confused. I want you to be quiet, and if you don't be quiet I'm going to get up and give you a whipping."

Like natural children, spiritual children have never learned the value of silence. We need to be careful about what we say.

There was a fellow called Father Nash who used to go along ahead of Charles Finney and get a few folks together to pray for the revival. Someone once asked Finney, "Do you know a little preacher by the name of Father Nash?"

Finney said, "Yes sir. He goes along ahead of time and prays for the revival. I don't have him hired. He just took it upon himself to do it."

"What kind of a fellow is he?" this person asked.

"Well," Finney said, "he's just like any other fellow who prays — he is a fellow of few words."

Folks who are talking all the time are usually guilty of at least three sins. They are often guilty of *evil speaking* — talking about and discussing the faults and failures of people not present. They are often guilty of *vain speaking* — always talking about themselves: what I've done; what I'm going to do; where I've been. And they are often guilty of *foolish speaking* — jesting, joking, and things that are unprofitable.

1. *Evil speaking — talking about and discussing the faults and failures of people not present.*

(We'll soon get through with this negative side of growing up and get on to the positive side. But this side needs to be dealt with, too.)

I was holding a meeting in Oklahoma when my son was about twelve. He had a four-day weekend holiday so I drove down to Texas and brought him back to spend a few days with me. I was gone all the time and didn't get to be with him much. We stayed in the parsonage with the pastor and his wife.

One day at the table, the pastor got to talking about some of the church members, airing some of their faults and failures. I noticed my boy just kept looking at him.

Finally I said to him, right at his own table, "Brother, I wish you wouldn't talk that way in front of my boy."

He looked at me rather startled.

I said, "I would rather you'd curse in front of him. That wouldn't register on him. He wouldn't pay any attention to that. But for the twelve years I pastored, he always thought every member we ever had was an angel."

They weren't — any more than all his members were. But Ken thought all of them were sprouting wings — he didn't know that was just their shoulder blades sticking out. He never heard his parents say one word about any deacon, Sunday School teacher, superintendent, or church member.

You need to be careful what you say around children, and other people as well.

I remember one dear soul. Bless her heart. Every time we took prayer requests she would say, "Pray for So-and-so," and she'd call her husband's name. He came with her every once in a while and even if he was there she'd never stop to think about it;

27

but would get up and call his name."

He rather liked me and I'd go visit him. We'd talk about the Bible. To tell you the real truth about it, he knew more about the Bible than she did. And in talking to him, I learned some things. I learned where she was missing it. I tried to talk to her about it, but it didn't help.

So one Wednesday night when there wasn't anyone there but us; when she said, "Pray for So-and-so," I said, "Sister, we're not going to do it."

I answered her right back from the pulpit and said, "We're not going to do it. Don't turn in another prayer request for him. We've prayed and prayed, but you undo all our prayers. You run home from church every single time some woman in the church looks a little hatefully at you — you think — and you tell your husband what an awful person she is. And if the preacher doesn't just preach to suit you, you run home and tell him what an awful person the preacher is. I know. I've talked to him. He couldn't have known it unless you told him. He knows more about what's going on down at this church than anyone in the church. You run home and tell him everything that is — and a lot of things that ain't. You rehash every-body's faults, failures, and shortcomings. And as long as you're going to do that, you're going to un-dermine the effects of our prayers."

I learned to appreciate that dear soul. She had enough sense to listen and she straightened up.

28

She became a splendid Christian. And he got saved. I dealt what seemed like severely with her, but she took it. She wasn't an ignoramus. People who do have a little something upstairs are able to know when you are telling them the truth. Some folks would never know and you just have to help them the best you can.

2. *Vain speaking — always talking about themselves.*

Sometimes I almost get sickened when I go to church. All the singing is about what I did, what I felt, and what happened. We scarcely worship the Lord. It's no wonder to me that God doesn't move any more than He does in our midst. The Bible said in the 13th chapter of Acts concerning this group down at Antioch, *"As they ministered to the Lord, and fasted, the Holy Ghost said,...."* (verse 2). They weren't ministering to one another.

If we can be humble enough and yielded enough God can use us. I just don't like the idea of leaving the impression we are something big and something great. It's all right to talk about how God uses people and rejoice about what God is doing. But I've been in some meetings where those in charge bragged on each other from the natural standpoint until it was simply nauseating.

Thank God for His blessings. And let's be careful that we are not taken up with vain talking.

3. *Foolish speaking.*

It's all right to be friendly. And it's all right to tell something funny sometimes — but it is possible to spend too much of your time doing that. The Bible even says something about jesting and joking that are not convenient. It doesn't say they are a sin necessarily, but it says they are not convenient.

> EPHESIANS 5:4
> 4 Neither filthiness, nor foolish talking, nor jesting, which are not convenient: but rather giving of thanks.

I was holding a meeting one time for a fellow, a fine fellow. I think a lot of him. He's changed considerably. But I never saw a fellow as full of jokes as he was then. We had two services a day, and every time I saw him he'd tell me a new joke. I don't see how in the world he could remember them. He'd tell me at least three a day which were brand new. Morning service, evening service, and when we'd go out for a bite to eat after church he'd have another one for me; sometimes several.

I usually quote my scripture as I preach and once when we were out eating he said, "I wish I could remember scriptures like you do."

I said, "You could if you'd spend as much time on them as you do on jokes. How do you remember jokes? I can't remember them. I go to tell some of them and get them all messed up."

The thing about it was I wasn't interested in

them.

Now don't go off and say I said it was wrong to tell something funny. I didn't say that at all. I said it is wrong to put that first and just blab, blab, blab, blab, and leave God out. I'm talking about things that will hinder our spiritual growth. We are never going to grow spiritually and just feed and talk on those kinds of things.

I'm a preacher and I fellowship with preachers more than anyone else. It's a strange thing, but sometimes in trying to fellowship with preachers you can't find too many you can really talk to about spiritual things. I've held meetings in church after church — Full Gospel churches — and preacher after preacher wants only to talk about fishing and hunting, or about how many cattle they have down on their ranch, or how many houses they have, or how much property they have. I think it's all right to go fishing. It's all right to go hunting. It's all right to have property. I'm glad they do. But if you'd try to mention the things of God and get in the least bit deep, they'd look at you like you were a nut.

I'm glad it's not that way with some folks. But it is that way with too many. And we cannot grow spiritually and spend all our time talking about natural things.

31

Chapter 4

MANHOOD

There are many scriptural characteristics of the manhood stage of spirituality. In fact, this entire book is aimed at seeing this spiritual man. But three of his characteristics we'll discuss here are:
1. Esteeming Earthly Things Lightly
2. Deadness to Censure or Praise
3. Ability to Recognize God at Work

Esteeming Earthly Things Lightly

> *"By faith Moses, when he was come to years, refused to be called the son of Pharaoh's*

daughter; Choosing rather to suffer affliction with the people of God, than to enjoy the pleasures of sin for a season; Esteeming the reproach of Christ greater riches than the treasures in Egypt: for he had respect unto the recompence of the reward."

-Hebrews 11:24-26

Moses, when he was come to years — that means when he grew up, when he became a man — refused to be called the son of Pharaoh's daughter.

Think about what he refused. He saw a difference in the people of God and the people of the world. (Egypt is a type of the world.) In the world he was the son of Pharaoh's daughter, in line for the throne. He had honor, wealth, prestige. He had the things the earth and the world had to offer. Yet he esteemed the reproach of Christ greater riches than the treasures in Egypt. Heir to the treasures of Egypt, but he esteemed the reproaches.

One characteristic of growing up is to esteem earthly things lightly. You cannot put earthly things above spiritual things and grow spiritually.

God wants to prosper His children. He's concerned about us. He wants us to have the good things of life. He said in His Word, "If ye be willing and obedient, ye shall eat the good of the land" (Isaiah 1:19). But He doesn't want us to put

34

those things first.

Some are more interested in making the dollar than in serving God. Spiritual things must come first if you are to be spiritual. You must esteem spiritual things more than the dollar, more than earthly things.

No, it's not wrong to have money. It's wrong for money to have you. It's wrong for money to be your ruler, your master.

God wants you to prosper.

III JOHN 2
2 Beloved, I wish above all things that thou mayest prosper and be in health, even as thy soul prospereth.

That's talking about financial and material prosperity, physical prosperity, and spiritual prosperity. Look at it again. "Beloved, I wish above all things that thou mayest prosper (material prosperity) and be in health (physical prosperity), even as thy soul (spiritual prosperity) prospereth."

The first Psalm is so beautiful — and makes it so clear that God wants us to prosper.

PSALM 1:1-3
1 Blessed is the man that walketh not in the counsel of the ungodly, nor standeth in the way of sinners, nor sitteth in

35

the seat of the scornful.

2   But his delight is in the law of the Lord; and in his law doth he meditate day and night.

3   And he shall be like a tree planted by the rivers of water, that bringeth forth his fruit in his season; his leaf also shall not wither; and whatsoever he doeth shall prosper.

God wants us to prosper.

Our need, however, is to evaluate things as they should be evaluated — to esteem earthly things lightly — to put first things first.

We all think the preacher ought to be that way. If a pastor takes a better church where he makes more money, people think, "He just took that so he'd be better paid." But they wouldn't think a thing in the world of taking a better job, and perhaps moving off and leaving a good spiritual church and getting in one where they'd all backslide.

I was talking to a fellow a number of years ago. I was over in his town on business and ran into him on the street. This was back in depression days. He had a good job, making good money, but he'd been offered a job making $50 more a month. That doesn't sound like much today, but in those low depression days it was a lot of money. I knew lots of men with families who didn't even make

36

$50 a month. He already made a good salary, but was offered this job in another town, making $50 more than he was making.

He said, "Did you know I was moving to So-and-so?"

He was a member of a Full Gospel church and I happened to know that in the town where he was moving they didn't have a Full Gospel church.

So I said, "What kind of church do you have in that town?"

He said, "What do you mean?"

I said, "Is there a Full Gospel church there?"

He said, "I don't know; I never thought about that."

I said, "No, you were just interested in the $50 more a month. But wait a minute, I knew you before you came into Pentecost. I happen to know you'd spent all your money. Doctors thought your wife had cancer of the stomach. But when she got the baptism of the Holy Ghost, without anybody praying for her, she got healed and can eat anything she wants. I happen to know you'd spent thousands of dollars on one of your boys physically, but since you've come in where divine healing is taught, that boy has been in good health."

He said, "Yes, that's right."

I said, "I happen to know that there isn't a Full Gospel church in that town."

(It would have been different if he was thinking

37

about going there to start one, but he wasn't capable.)

He said, "You know, I never thought of that."

I said, "No, you'd take your family out of a good church where the Gospel is preached, where you've been blessed immeasurably, physically as well as spiritually, for $50 more a month. I'll not tell you to go or not to go, but I will tell you you'd better pray about it."

The next time I saw him, he said, "I'm not going. I don't believe it's worth it."

A man and his wife came to a meeting I was holding in Dallas. The woman's mother, who had gone to be with the Lord, was a member of a church I'd pastored some years before. She was a wonderful Christian and a great blessing to my wife and me as young people with babies.

I knew that this lady hadn't always been a Christian. She used to visit her mother and her mother said she wasn't saved. But then she had gotten saved, received the Holy Spirit, and attended an independent Full Gospel church; a fine church. And she was going on for God.

So I asked, "Where do you go to church now?"

She said, "Oh, I don't go anywhere."

"What do you mean? I thought you were a member of ..." And I mentioned a certain church.

"Oh, they don't even have a church there anymore. It was closed down for awhile. Then someone took it over. Our pastor backslid and quit

38

preaching. We don't go anywhere; just here and there. While you're here we're coming over here."

I said, "Where do you pay your tithes?"

"Oh, we quit. We used to pay tithes, but we don't anymore. We used to pay tithes to our pastor, but he backslid."

I said, "There's no use in your backsliding just because he did." I don't know whether they appreciated it or not, but I said, "You need to get in somewhere and work for God, and worship the Lord. A rolling stone never gathers any moss, as we say."

We need each other. We need the fellowship of one another.

Someone said, "Oh Brother Hagin, I can stay at home and be as good a Christian as anybody."

You can't do it. The Bible says, "Not forsaking the assembling of ourselves together, as the manner of some is; but exhorting one another: and so much the more, as ye see the day approaching" (Hebrews 10:25).

We see that day approaching — the coming of the Lord. We need one another. We need to grow up. We need to esteem earthly things lightly. We need to put God first.

We don't go to church because we're in love with the pastor or the wife of the pastor, or the Sunday School teacher. We should go because we love God and want to worship Him.

People sometimes lose their children because

they don't put first things first. The children grow up physically and get away from God, because the wrong example was set for them.

We were visiting my wife's folks in Sherman, Texas one Christmas when my daughter was only six years old. Christmas was on Saturday. The next day was Sunday. I was to preach about fifty-seven miles away. It was raining and disagreeable. When you'd get out it would seem to go right through you.

Sunday morning my mother-in-law said, "I'll keep Pat. Just leave her here. She has a hacking cough and it feels like she may have a little bit of fever."

I said, "No, we're not going to leave her. We prayed and believed God. And besides that when we came over here yesterday she had that same little hacking cough. Actually she's much better today. If we don't take her to Sunday School and church this morning, then we'll leave the impression on a little six year old that it's more important to eat Christmas dinner with Grandma than to go to church on Sunday morning. And that's not what I believe."

Do you see where people lose their children? And why they grow up and become unfaithful in church?

You can't just tell them. The Bible says, "Train up a child in the way he should go: and when he is old, he will not depart from it" (Proverbs 22:6).

40

F.F. Bosworth said, "Some people wonder why they can't have faith for healing. They feed their body three hot meals a day, and their spirit one cold snack a week."

Determine in your heart to put spiritual things first. First things first. Esteem earthly things lightly, even if it's your own relatives. Put God before them. Put God before your own self-life. You will be blessed spiritually, and better off physically — both you and your family as well.

Deadness to Censure or Praise

> "But with me it is a very small thing that I should be judged of you, or of man's judgment: yea, I judge not mine own self. For I know nothing by myself; yet am I not hereby justified: but he that judgeth me is the Lord."
>
> -I Corinthians 4:3-4

Paul had grown in grace to such an extent that he sought only to commend himself to God. He was not influenced or affected by what others thought of him. He did not get in bondage to anybody. It was not a carnal independence — but a saintly dignity.

The law of love governed him. He was not easily puffed up, nor was he touchy or resentful. His spirit — where the love of God was shed

41

abroad — dominated him.

Immature Christians will feel slighted or puffed up. If they are criticized — or even imagine that they are — they are restless, uneasy, and full of self-pity. On the other hand, if they are noticed and appreciated they feel lifted up and full of self-importance.

Baby Christians are *self*-conscious. And ever-conscious of what others are thinking about them. Therefore they are "tossed to and fro" childishly trying to be popular.

The mature believer is *God*-conscious. And ever-conscious of what God's Word says about him and to him. Because he is able to testify with Paul, "It is a *very small thing* that I should be judged of you or man's judgment," he is free to walk in and voice his convictions.

He fits the description given in the Amplified translation of I Corinthians 13:5. He is not conceited — arrogant and inflated with pride. He is not touchy or fretful or resentful. He takes no account of the evil done to him — pays no attention to a suffered wrong.

Ability to Recognize God at Work

One of the best spiritual examples of this characteristic is Joseph.

You remember how he saw certain things happening in a dream and his brothers became jealous of him. They were going to kill him, but finally just sold him into slavery. He was taken into Egypt, where eventually he stood and refused to bow to the wishes of his master's wife and was thrown into prison. He stayed in prison seven years.

Most people would have become bitter and said, "God has forsaken me after these seven years."

He interpreted a dream for a fellow prisoner — Pharaoh's butler — that in three days the butler would be lifted up and restored. Joseph asked the butler to make mention of him to Pharaoh when he was delivered. The butler was released as Joseph said, but he forgot Joseph. It was two years more before Joseph got out.

In those two years most folks would have grown bitter saying, "That's the way it is. You try to help folks and they won't help you."

But the time came when Joseph was brought out of prison. And eventually he was made prime minister of Egypt.

A famine back in his home country caused his father to send his brothers to Egypt in search of food. They had to be brought before him because he was prime minister.

They didn't know him. But he recognized them; the very ones who had sold him into slavery. He didn't tell them who he was but asked, "Is

43

your father well, the old man of whom ye spake?"
They answered that he was in good health.

Benjamin hadn't come with them. So Joseph
said to them, "Hereby ye shall be proved: By the
life of Pharaoh ye shall not go forth hence, except
your youngest brother come hither."

They went back and told their father, "The
man did solemnly protest unto us, saying, Ye shall
not see my face, except your brother be with you."

Poor old Jacob didn't know that it was God.
Joseph was gone. And now they were taking Benjamin. He thought all things were against him.
But they weren't. They were all for him. He just
didn't know it.

When you're hungry, you'll do about anything,
so Benjamin went with them. When they got
there, Joseph made a feast for them. And he an-
nounced, "I am Joseph."

Do you know what happened?

All those fellows hit the floor. That's what
Joseph had seen in his dream — his brothers bow-
ing before him.

Here would have been a fine opportunity for
most people, who weren't spiritually mature and
still babies, to have really shown off. Here would
have been a perfect opportunity for Joseph to have
stuck his thumbs in his galluses and said, "Well
boys, look me over. Remember those dreams I
had? They came to pass."

But Joseph had magnanimity of soul. He said in

effect, "Don't worry about it, God did it." He said, "Be not grieved, nor angry with yourselves, that ye sold me hither: for God did send me before you to preserve you a posterity in the earth, and to save your lives by a great deliverance" (Genesis 45:5, 7).

When you can see God at work in things, you can rejoice whatever is going on!

PART II

Chapter 5

WALKING WITH YOUR FATHER

"Therefore I say unto you, Take no thought for your life, what ye shall eat, or what ye shall drink; nor yet for your body, what ye shall put on. Is not the life more than meat, and the body than raiment?

Behold the fowls of the air: for they sow not, neither do they reap, nor gather into barns; yet your heavenly Father feedeth them. Are ye not much better than they?

Which of you by taking thought can add one cubit unto his stature?

And why take ye thought for raiment? Consider the lilies of the field, how they grow; they toil not, neither do they spin:

And yet I say unto you, That even Solomon in all his glory was not arrayed like one of these.

Wherefore, if God so clothe the grass of the field, which today is, and to-morrow is cast into the oven, shall he not much more clothe you, O ye of little faith?

Therefore take no thought, saying, What shall we eat? or, What shall we drink? or, Wherewithal shall we be clothed?

(For after all these things do the Gentiles seek:) for your heavenly Father knoweth that ye have need of all these things.

But seek ye first the kingdom of God, and his righteousness; and all these things shall be added unto you.

Take therefore no thought for the morrow: for the morrow shall take thought for the things of itself. Sufficient unto the day is the evil thereof."

-Matthew 6:25-34

This is a marvelous section of scripture. But for the time being there are just two portions of it I want you to notice. In the 32nd verse, *"for your heavenly Father knoweth that ye have need of all these things."* And in the 26th verse, *"your heavenly Father feedeth them."*

48

This isn't talking about sinners (unbelievers) here, because He is not the heavenly Father of sinners. To listen to some people talk we are all children of God; God is the Father of all of us, and we're all brothers and sisters. But no, we are not. The devil is the father of some people.

Jesus said to some of the most religious people of that day, "Ye are of your father the devil" (John 8:44). He didn't say our heavenly Father was their father. He said the devil was their father.

Yet even though we have been born-again, and have become children of God, I think so many times we have never really become acquainted with our Father. Our theme is growing — growing up spiritually. We need to grow by becoming acquainted with our heavenly Father.

When I was teaching down in East Texas on this subject a woman said to me, "Brother Hagin, I've been saved for eleven years. And ever since I've been saved I've loved Jesus. But somehow I just didn't become acquainted with the Father like I should. Since you've been teaching along this line though, I have become acquainted with my Heavenly Father. And I'm just about to love Him to death."

That was her expression.

There is no truth in all the Bible as far reaching as the blessed fact that if we have been born-again and come into the family of God, God the Father is our Father, and He cares for us.

49

He is interested in us. I mean in each one of us individually; not just as a group, or a body, or a church. He is interested in each of His children and He loves every single one of us with the same love.

Jesus was actually preaching here in Matthew to the Jews. Yet one reason they didn't understand Him was, He talked about God as being His Father. He endeavored to introduce to them a kind, loving, Heavenly Father. They couldn't understand that kind of a God. His message was, "For God so loved the world that He gave...." They couldn't comprehend it.

The Old Covenant was the covenant of the law of sin and death. It was the law of an eye for an eye and a tooth for a tooth. You knock my eye out and I'll knock your eye out.

It was the law where God demanded, in awful judgment, love and so forth. They were not able to do it because their natures had not been changed. So He set up the Levitical priesthood whereby the blood of animals could be shed to cover their sins so they could be counted righteous in His sight and He could bless them. The sins of the people could be confessed over the head of the scapegoat. The goat let go in the wilderness. And judgment fell out there instead of on them. They had come up in this hard, harsh atmosphere of justice.

When God gave Moses the tables of stone of the

50

law, fire and vapor of smoke overshadowed the mountain. If even an animal touched it he was thrust through with a sword.

In the Old Testament after they built the tabernacle first and the temple secondly, they didn't know Him as Father God. They knew Him as Elohim, or Jehovah. They did not know Him personally. They had no personal acquaintance with Him. His Presence was kept shut up in the Holy of Holies. It was necessary that every male throughout Israel, at least once a year, go up to Jerusalem to the temple to present himself before God. That's where He was. And even then they didn't dare enter into His Presence.

No one entered His Presence save the high priest. And he only under great precaution. For if you intruded into that place in the wrong way, and some did, you fell down dead instantly. This high priest, after offering sacrifice by the blood of animals for his own sins and the sins of the people, could enter into the Holy of Holies and receive atonement for their sins — pushing them off, so to speak, into the future.

That was the hard, harsh atmosphere they had come up in. It is no wonder that when Jesus came along to introduce them to a loving, kind, Heavenly Father, they couldn't understand it.

But I'm afraid that is not only true concerning those Jews — I'm afraid it is true concerning the sons and daughters of Almighty God today. They

51

have never really become acquainted with Him as being their Father.

Here are some of the things Jesus said about the Father.

"And in that day ye shall ask me nothing. Verily, verily, I say unto you, Whatsoever ye shall ask the Father in my name, he will give it you" (John 16:23).

"For the Father himself loveth you...." (John 16:27).

"...for your Father knoweth what things ye have need of, before ye ask him. After this manner therefore pray ye: Our Father...." (Matthew 6:8-9). Notice the utter tenderness of it, "Our Father...."

I like something Paul said when he prayed for the church at Ephesus. He began his prayer like this, "For this cause I bow my knees unto the Father of our Lord Jesus Christ, of whom the whole family in heaven and earth is named" (Ephesians 3:14-15).

Oh, I like to do that. I like to get on my knees and repeat those words of Paul, "I bow my knees unto the Father of our Lord Jesus Christ, of whom the whole family in heaven and earth is named." That makes it so real. It takes it out of a hard, harsh religious atmosphere. This isn't religion. It hasn't a thing in the world to do with religion.

Some folks say, "Do you have religion?"

Thank God, I don't have a bit of it. I don't want any. When it's religion, it's "God" — but when it's family, it's "Father."

He may be "God" to the sinner, but He's

52

"Father" to me. "I bow my knees unto the Father of our Lord Jesus Christ, of whom the whole family...." It becomes the Father and His family! We are in the family of God. *It's not important what church you are in — the thing that's important is what family you are in.*

Getting Acquainted Through the Word

I'm glad I'm in His family. I want to become better acquainted with my Father, don't you? I want to know Him better, don't you? Thank God, we can.

How? How can we know more about Him? How can we become better acquainted with our Father?

I like something Smith Wigglesworth said, "I can't understand God by feelings. I understand God the Father by what the Word says about Him. He is everything the Word says He is. Get acquainted with the Father through the Word."

It is in the Word that we find out about Him, about His love, about His nature, about how He cares for us, about how He loves us. Jesus himself said, "Man shall not live by bread alone — (How shall he live?) — but by every word that proceedeth out of the mouth of God."

53

MATTHEW 6:26

26 Behold the fowls of the air: for they sow not, neither do they reap, nor gather into barns; yet your heavenly Father feedeth them. Are ye not much better than they?

The folks Jesus was preaching to never grasped it. It was new to them. It's almost new to us. We've never grasped it, because most of us have been taught to fear and shrink from a God of justice. We have never seen the love side of God that Jesus came to bring us.

MATTHEW 6:30-31

30 Wherefore, if God so clothe the grass of the field, which today is, and to-morrow is cast into the oven, shall he not much more clothe you, O ye of little faith?

31 Therefore take no thought, saying, What shall we eat? or, What shall we drink? or, Wherewithal shall we be clothed?

One translation says, "Be therefore not faithless saying, What shall we eat? or, What shall we drink?...." When you talk that way you are without faith.

MATTHEW 6:32-33

32 (For after all these things do the Gentiles seek;) for your heavenly Father knoweth that ye have need of all these things.

33 But seek ye first the kingdom of God, and his righteousness; and all these things shall be added unto you.

They won't be taken from you — they'll be added to you! This proves the Father cares for His own.

MATTHEW 6:34

34 Take therefore no thought for the morrow: for the morrow shall take thought for the things of itself. Sufficient unto the day is the evil thereof.

I like the translation that reads, "Be not anxious for the morrow." Sometimes you do have to think about tomorrow to make an appointment or plan something. Really the thought He's trying to get over is, "Don't worry about tomorrow." God doesn't want His children full of worry. He doesn't want us full of fretting. Why? Because He loves us.

Your Heavenly Father knoweth that you have need of these things. So have no worry, no fret, no anxiety. If He is your Father, you can be assured He will take a father's place and will perform a

55

father's part. You may be certain that if He is your Father, He loves you, and He will care for you.

> JOHN 14:21-23
> 21 He that hath my commandments, and keepeth them, he it is that loveth me: and he that loveth me shall be loved of my Father, and I will love him, and will manifest myself to him.
> 22 Judas saith unto him, not Iscariot, Lord, how is it that thou wilt manifest thyself unto us, and not unto the world?
> 23 Jesus answered and said unto him, If a man love me, he will keep my words: and my Father will love him, and we will come unto him, and make our abode with him.

Here we have the revelation of the Father's attitude toward His own children. Two things are emphasized:

1. *That you keep my commandments.* What are Jesus' commandments? He said, "A new commandment I give unto you, That ye love one another; as I have loved you...." (John 13:34). That sums it up. There's no use worrying about any other commandments for "...love is the fulfilling of the law" (Romans 13:10). If you keep Jesus' commandments, you will have fulfilled all the rest of the commandments.

2. *You shall be loved of my Father.* If you walk in love, you walk in God's realm, for God is Love. (We'll go into the love-walk further in chapter six.) The great Father God is a love God. His very nature — because He is Love — compels Him to care for us, protect us, and shield us.

> MATTHEW 7:11
> 11 If ye then, being evil, know how to give good gifts unto your children, how much more shall your Father which is in heaven give good things to them that ask him?

How much more! That sends a thrill through my spirit. How much more! Are you a parent? Would you have it as your plan, purpose and will that your children go through life poverty-stricken, nose-to-the-grindstone, sick, afflicted, downtrodden, downcast, down-and-out? No! Parents will sacrifice because they love their children. They'll work and sacrifice to help their children gain an education so they can have things better in life than they had. They want to shield them, because they love them, from some of the bumps and knocks and hard times they had. Just natural folks are that way. That's what Jesus said. "If ye then, being evil (or natural)...."

Our relationship as sons and daughters is a challenge to His love. *We hold the same relationship*

57

to the Father that Jesus did when He walked on earth.

JOHN 17:23
23 I in them, and thou in me, that they may be made perfect in one; and that the world may know that thou hast sent me, and hast loved them, as thou hast loved me.

The Father loves us just as He loved Jesus! And if He loves me as He loves Jesus, I'm not afraid to face life's problems. For He is with me as He was with the Master.

JOHN 16:32
32 Behold, the hour cometh, yea, is now come, that ye shall be scattered, every man to his own, and shall leave me alone: and yet I am not alone, because the Father is with me.

You and I can say, "I am not alone, because the Father is with me." For if He loves me as He loved Jesus, then He's with me as He was with Jesus. I am not alone.

JOHN 16:27
27 For the Father himself loveth you, because ye have loved me, and have believed that I came out from God.

Nothing can be stronger or more comforting than this fact: *The Father Himself knows you, and He loves you, and He longs to bless you.*

Against the background of all these statements Jesus made relative to the Father, other scriptures take on new light; they become immediately more real to us.

I PETER 5:7
7 Casting all your care upon him; for he careth for you.

This is a message from the very heart of the Father God to me, to you. He wants us to end worry — to end fear and doubt. You might say, "Can I do it?" Certainly. "How?" By casting all your care upon Him. He wants you to abandon yourself to His love and His care so He said, "Casting all your care upon Him, for He careth for you." Or, as the Amplified translation reads, and I love this, "Casting the whole of your care — all your anxieties, all your worries, all your concerns, once and for all — on Him; for He cares for you affectionately, and cares about you watchfully."

PHILIPPIANS 4:6
6 Be careful for nothing; but in every thing by prayer and supplication with thanksgiving let your requests be made known unto God.

59

Again, the Amplified translation says, "Do not fret or have any anxiety about anything,....." That's our Father speaking to us. Our Heavenly Father wants to walk with us just as He walked with Jesus when He was here on the earth.

PHILIPPIANS 4:13
13 I can do all things through Christ which strengtheneth me.

Some have said, "Yes, but Paul said that and he was an Apostle." Paul didn't say he could do all things because he was an Apostle. He said he could do all things through Christ. Paul wasn't in Christ any more than I am in Christ, or any more than you are in Christ. It was Christ who strengthened him. And the Father is just as real — if we let Him be — to us as He was to Paul, or even to Jesus. And He's sending a message from His heart of Love to you and me. He's telling us: You can do anything. You can rise to the place where you're unafraid in the most unpleasant circumstances because you know that your Father is on your side. "If God be for us, who can be against us?" (Romans 8:31).

The Father's love — and remember He is Love — compels Him to care for us. When you come to know His love and to swing free in that love, then all doubts and fears will be destroyed.

60

PSALM 27:1
1   The Lord is my light and my salvation; whom shall I fear? the Lord is the
strength of my life; of whom shall I be
afraid?

When you remember it is this wonderful
Heavenly Father who loves us even as He loved
Jesus, then you can understand that we need not
be afraid, even as Jesus was not afraid. He is your
Light. He is your Deliverance. (Salvation in this
verse means deliverance.) He is the Strength of
your life. Light! Deliverance! Strength! Then
there's nothing to fear. What can man do to the
man whom God loves and protects?

HEBREWS 13:5-6
5   ...for he hath said, I will never leave
thee, nor forsake thee.
6   So that we may boldly say, The Lord
is my helper, and I will not fear what
man shall do unto me.

He's your Helper! And He will meet your needs!

PHILIPPIANS 4:19
19 But my God shall supply all your
need according to his riches in glory by
Christ Jesus.

61

This is not religion. It's not preaching. It's a living truth from the heart of our wonderful, lovely, Father God to us. He wants us to know that He will supply all our needs according to *His riches* in glory by Christ Jesus.

Experiencing Acquaintance

PSALM 23:1-6
1   The Lord is my shepherd; I shall not want.
2   He maketh me to lie down in green pastures: he leadeth me beside the still waters.
3   He restoreth my soul: he leadeth me in the paths of righteousness for his name's sake.
4   Yea, though I walk through the valley of the shadow of death, I will fear no evil: for thou art with me; thy rod and thy staff they comfort me.
5   Thou preparest a table before me in the presence of mine enemies: thou anointest my head with oil; my cup runneth over.
6   Surely goodness and mercy shall follow me all the days of my life: and I will dwell in the house of the Lord for ever.

To me, no passage describes the love-attitude of

62

the Father and Jesus toward us more beautifully than the 23rd Psalm.

Many Psalms are prophetic. The 22nd Psalm is a picture of Jesus dying. In the 23rd Psalm He is the Good Shepherd. The 24th Psalm shows Him as the coming King of kings and Lord of lords upon this earth.

We are living in the 23rd Psalm right now. "The Lord is my shepherd." When Jesus came He said, "I am (present tense) the good shepherd." Romans 10:9 says, "That if thou shalt confess with thy mouth the Lord Jesus, (or, Jesus as Lord)...." The Lord is my shepherd. Now. We live in the 23rd Psalm.

This is my interpretation of the 23rd Psalm, I always say it this way: "The Lord is my shepherd, I do not want." I do not want. Perfect satisfaction. The ultimate of living.

Verse 2 is where the luscious clover and tender grass carpet the ground. No effort on my part is required to have or to get enough.

He leads me beside the water, waters of stillness. Water and food are the requisites that sustain life. Thank God, He leads me, He leadeth me, He supplies every need.

He makes me lie down and rest in safety and quietness in the pastures of plenty. Near me is a babbling brook. Its Living Waters answer the cry of my heart. I have water. I have food. I have protection. I have shelter. I have His care. This is my

Father.

When I am frightened and filled with fear, when my whole being is convulged with agony, He restoreth my soul. He keeps me quiet. He makes me normal again. He brushes away my fears and anxieties, holds me to His breast, and breathes into me courage and faith.

My heart laughs at my enemies, for He guideth me down the paths of grace through the realm of righteousness where I stand in His Presence as though sin had never been; and romp and play in the throne room of grace with never a thought, nor a fear, nor a dread. My Father, you see, is the One who is on the throne.

He may be Judge to the world, and God to the sinner, but He's Father to me.

And sometimes I come in, most of the time in fact to visit with Him and I hear Him say, "Son, is there anything you want? What can I do for you?"

And I say, "Father, I don't want a thing. You're so wonderful, and so lovely, and so good you've already provided for me all I'll ever need. And you wrote me a letter and told me about it. So I don't have a care. I don't have a need. I don't have a want that hasn't been met. No, I didn't come for something. I'll tell you, Father, I just came in to visit with you for awhile. I just wanted to hang around the throne. I like to be near you, Father."

My Father said to me (Oh, I could hear His voice so plainly as He spoke to me), "Son, you don't know how that delights my heart. No earthly father ever desired the companionship and the fellowship of his children any more than I, the Heavenly Father, desire the fellowship and companionship of my children.

"You know," He said to me, "I made man so I'd have someone to fellowship with. I made man for my companion. In fact, I'll put it this way (and He said it in just these words), I made man so I'd have someone to pal with. I put Adam on the earth in the garden, and in the cool of the day, I'd go down and walk and talk with him."

It is so blessed and so beautiful and so wonderful to be able to walk with God.

Chapter 6

WALKING IN LOVE

"...the love of God is shed abroad in our hearts by the Holy Ghost...."
                                        -Romans 5:5

To fellowship with God, to walk with God, to walk in God's realm, we must walk in love. Divine Love. For God is Love.

When I was born-again, He became my Father. He is a Love God. I am a Love child of a Love God. I'm born of God, and God is Love, so I am born of Love. The nature of God is in me. And the nature of God is Love.

We can't say we don't have this Divine Love.

Everyone in the family has it, or else they're not in the family. They may not be exercising it. They may be like the one-talent guy that wrapped his talent in a napkin and buried it. But the Bible says that the Love of God has been shed abroad in our hearts by the Holy Ghost. That means the *God-kind of Love* has been shed abroad in our hearts, our spirits. This is a Love family.

Jesus said, "By this shall all men know that ye are my disciples — (How are they going to know it?) — if ye have love one to another" (John 13:35). That's the way they're going to know us.

This kind of Love is not selfish. "God so loved the world that he gave...."

The love law of the family of God is. "That ye love one another; as I have loved you," (John 13:34). How did He love us? Because we deserved it? No! He loved us while we were yet unlovely. He loved us while we were yet sinners. The Bible says so.

(And think about this. If God loved us with so great love when we were sinners, when we were unlovely, when we were His enemies, do you think He loves His children any less? No, a thousand times no.)

"Loves" Compared: Divine — Natural Human

This Love we're talking about is Divine Love, not natural human love. We hear a lot today about

68

natural human love, but there is simply no love in this old world like the Love of God. Natural human love is selfish. I've heard people say, "A mother's love is akin to the love of God." I thought that at one time. But it isn't so. As a usual thing a mother's love is a natural human love. And as a usual thing, it's selfish. "That's *my* baby."

"Oh, I love my children, I love them," a woman came crying to me saying, "I want you to pray for them. I've brought them up right here in this church, and I don't understand it. Not a one of them will come except my girl."

One of her daughters played the piano and she was the only one who came. In fact, one of the boys had just run away from home.

She said, "There isn't anyone in this church that loved their children any more than I did."

I said, "Sister, there has to be a reason. I'm a stranger here, just an evangelist, but I can see this poor girl here on the piano bench. You've smothered her with your 'love.' And I'll guarantee the reason the rest of them ran off is because you wouldn't let them out from under your coattail. You wanted to run their lives entirely. (I'd look at this girl at the piano and she'd duck her head. She didn't know how to act.) I dare say your daughter has never had a boy friend in her life, or a girl friend either."

"Well no," she said, "I just always kept her at home. I thought I could raise her up better."

69

I said, "No, you couldn't. Her personality is twisted."

Natural human mother love; but it was selfish. She didn't have her children's interests at heart. She had her interests at heart. She wanted to keep them with her.

Have you ever noticed that mothers-in-law rarely have trouble with sons-in-law? It's usually with daughters-in-law. Many times that mother just feels there is no girl anywhere good enough for "my boy." Oh yes, she may be saved, filled with the Holy Ghost, and talking in tongues every night, but instead of letting the Love of God in her heart dominate her, she is letting the natural human love in her flesh dominate her. Constantly picking. Constantly saying things.

The reason mother-in-law and daughter-in-law have trouble — if they don't walk in Love — is that for years that mother was the main one in the life of this boy. She wants to keep on telling him what to do. And now the wife wants to tell him what to do. They can't both tell him what to do. And he's in a dilemma.

The Love of God is in our hearts, but it may be like the talent that was wrapped in a napkin and hidden in the earth. We may not use it, but that Love of God is in our hearts.

If we would use it, and learn to let that love dominate us, it would make a difference in our lives. It would cure the ills in our homes. This kind of Love has never been to a divorce court, and will never go. It was natural human love that went there. Natural human love can turn to hatred when it doesn't get its way. It will fight and fuss, claw and knock, cuss and be mean. Divine Love, when it is reviled, revileth not again. I didn't say Christians haven't been to a divorce court; they have. But they weren't letting the Love of God dominate them.

God wants us to grow. And thank God, we can grow in Love. The Bible speaks of being made perfect, or mature, in Love. No, we haven't been made perfect in Love yet, but we can be and some of us are on our way.

The God-kind of Love is not interested in what I can get — but in what I can give. Do you see how that can solve all the problems in your home?

Too many are selfish. And even though they are Christians, they let the natural dominate them. "What can I get." "I'm not going to take this." "I'm not going to take that." "I'm not going to put up with this." "I." "I." "I." "I."

It's true in churches. In the second church I pastored I was twenty and single so I rented a room from a couple in the church. The man knew the Bible and had a marvelous experience with God. But he was the type that said, "I've got my say-so, and I'm going to have it. I'm a member of that church just as much as anyone else and I've got my say-so." He had his say-so, and so did some

71

others, until everything was wrecked.

I only stayed six months. God told me to tell them that unless they repented the time would come when they wouldn't have a church. Through the first prophetic utterance I ever had He said, "I'll remove their candlestick. If they don't repent, the doors of this church will be closed within one year. They will remain closed two years, and then they will open up again. I'll give them one more chance. If they don't make it then, this church building will be moved off this church lot."

They got mad. They were about ready to do to me the same thing those folks were ready to do to Jesus in His hometown of Nazareth. They were ready to throw Him off the brow of the hill. They reported what I'd said to some of the elders of the movement, and they wanted to boot me out, but were a little afraid to.

However, at the end of the year, just as He said, the doors of that church closed for two years. A padlock was on it. Then a fellow opened it up again. And God gave them a certain amount of time. But they didn't walk in the light and it shut down. It came to pass just as God said. I could take you there and show you a lot with no church today, and it still belongs to that particular movement.

Through the years there were enough of them to have a church. But they couldn't. Because they

72

couldn't get along among themselves. They never got above the babyhood stage of Christianity. They remained babies. They didn't grow.

As children of God the nature of God is in us. And God's nature is Love. So it is natural for us, spiritually, to Love. But if I let my outward man and my mind dominate me, that Love nature in my heart is kept prisoner. Let's release the Love of God that's within us.

An Expose' on Love

What about this God-kind of Love? What are its characteristics? They're given to us in I Corinthians 13. It is to be regretted that the King James translates the Greek word for divine love, *agape,* as charity. My favorite translation of this "Expose' on Love" is the Amplified. Let's look into it in the Amplified beginning with verse 4:

> *"Love endures long and is patient and kind;"*
> A lot of people endure long — but they aren't patient and kind while they do it. They just suffer long because they have to. "I've suffered all I'm going to. I'm not going to have it this way any more."

> *"Love never is envious nor boils over with jealousy;"*
> It's natural human love that is jealous. This kind of love doesn't boil over with jealousy.

73

"Love is not boastful or vainglorious, does not display itself haughtily. It is not conceited — arrogant and inflated with pride; it is not rude (unmannerly), and does not act unbecomingly."

"Love (God's love in us) does not insist on its own rights or its own way, for it is not self-seeking;"

I wish you would take time to let that soak in. "Well, I know what's mine though. I've got my say-so and I'm going to have it. I've got my rights and I'm going to have them." No matter how much they may hurt someone else.

This says Love doesn't insist on its own rights. We'll never make it until we start believing in God, and believing in Love. It's the best way! And it's your way!

"(Love) is not touchy or fretful or resentful; it takes no account of the evil done to it — pays no attention to a suffered wrong."

Here is the Love thermometer. Here is the Love gauge. It's very easy to find out whether or not you're walking in Love. When you begin to take account of the evil done to you, you're not walking in Love. As long as you walk in God and stay full of the Spirit, you won't take account of the evil done to you.

74

Through the years things have happened to me, just as they have to you. And I've had ministers, and even relatives tell me, "I wouldn't take that. I wouldn't put up with that. Not me." But I just kept my mouth shut and never said a word, smiled and stayed happy. Why? I wouldn't take time to deny it if they told on me I killed my grandma. I'd just keep shouting, "Hallelujah! Praise God! Glory to God!" Just go on. You'll come out on top in the long run.

Even ministers have told me, "There must be a weakness in your character. You never take up for yourself." No, it's a strength. Because Love never fails. Many have failed; and have even died prematurely because they lived so in the natural they couldn't take advantage of the privileges and rights of a child of God which belonged to them. They were always fussing and fighting until it had an effect on their bodies.

"(Love) takes no account of the evil done to it."

That has to be the God-kind of Love because we were enemies of God, and God didn't take account of the evil we had done to Him. He sent Jesus to redeem us. He loved us while we were yet sinners.

"(Love) pays no attention to a suffered wrong."

As an old boy down in Georgia said, "You might as well come up to the licklog and admit it's so," there aren't too many people walking in Love — in God's Love, in Christ's Love — even though they have it. They're walking in natural human love. And they sure pay attention to a suffered wrong. They get all puffed. A husband and wife, both Christians, will get mad and won't speak for a week because of some wrong. I know I'm on your toes, but I just want to stand there a while.

Can't you see how it would straighten things out for us in the home, the church, the nation, for men to become children of God and get the Love of God in them, and then live in the family of God as children of God?

"(Love) does not rejoice at injustice and unrighteousness, but rejoices when right and truth prevail."

"Love bears up under anything and everything that comes."

Someone said, "I just can't take it any longer." Love can. "I just can't put up with

76

him any longer." Think about God. He's putting up with all of us. "I've taken just about all I can take." That's old natural human love. The Love of God in you bears up under everything.

"(Love) is ever ready to believe the best of every person."

Natural human love is ready to believe the worst of every person. It's ever ready to believe the worst about the husband, the worst about the wife, the worst about the children. But this God-kind of Love is ever ready to believe the best of every person; husband, wife, brother or sister in the church, children. Believe the best of every person.

I've traveled across the country in the ministry. It's amazing what you hear on this preacher and that preacher, this person and that person, this deacon and that deacon, this Sunday School teacher and that Sunday School teacher, this singer and that singer. I never pay the least bit of attention to any of them. I don't believe a word of it. I believe the best of everyone.

Children ought to have the right to be brought up in this kind of a Love atmosphere. They'll go out in life's fight and win then. But when you see the worst in your children, always telling them, "You'll never amount to anything. You won't do this and you won't do that," they'll live up to what you say. Though they may have missed it, when you see the best in them and love them rightly it will bring the best out of them. They will amount to something.

"(Love's) hopes are fadeless under all circumstances and it endures everything (without weakening). Love never fails — never fades out or becomes obsolete or comes to an end."
If you walk in love you will not fail. Love never fails!

We are interested in spiritual gifts and we ought to be. But we ought to be interested in Love first. Prophecies will fail. Tongues shall cease. Knowledge shall vanish away. But, thank God, Love never fails.

Oh yes, I believe in prophecy and prophesying. I believe in tongues. Thank God for it. But you can exercise these things outside of Love and they become as sounding brass and tinkling cymbal.

The thing about it is: Let's have prophecy. Let's have tongues. Let's have faith. Let's have knowledge. But let's have Love with it. Let's put Love first because we are in the family of Love and have become acquainted with our Heavenly Father who is a God of Love.

We ought to want to learn. We ought to want to grow. We ought to want to grow in Love until we are made perfect in Love. I haven't been made perfect in love yet, have you? But did you know the Bible says we can? Not in the next world, but in this world. I believe some of us are going to make it. I'm not going to quit just because I haven't made it yet. I'm going to keep after it. Thank God for His Word! Thank God for His Love!

PART III

Chapter 7

RECEIVING THE KNOWLEDGE

*"Till we all come in the unity of the faith,
and of the knowledge of the Son of God, unto
a perfect man...."*

-Ephesians 4:13

How is that going to come about?

I guess we all want to be mature spiritually, but just wanting to be doesn't make it so. How are we to grow spiritually?

We've already pointed out I Peter 2:2, "As newborn babes, desire the sincere milk of the word, that ye may grow thereby." God starts us in the spiritual, just like folks get started in the natural. When babies are born they start off on milk. They certainly couldn't eat meat. And God says that this sincere milk of the Word will cause us to grow.

Yet there are some things Paul wrote to the Corinthian Christians and to the Hebrew Christians which are of interest to us.

I CORINTHIANS 3:1-2

1   And I, brethren, could not speak unto you as unto spiritual, but as unto carnal, even as unto babes in Christ.

2   I have fed you with milk, and not with meat: for hitherto ye were not able to bear it, neither yet now are ye able.

HEBREWS 5:11-14 (Comments in parentheses)

11 Of whom we have many things to say, and hard to be uttered, seeing ye are dull of hearing. (Some things are hard to get over to folks because they are dull of hearing.)

12 For when for the time ye ought to be teachers, ye have need that one teach you again which be the first principles of the oracles of God; and are become such as have need of milk, and not of strong meat.

13 For every one that useth milk is

unskilful in the word of righteousness
(The margin reads 'hath no experience in
the word of righteousness.' Now why has
he no experience in the word of righteousness?): for he is a babe.
14 But strong meat belongeth to them
that are of full age (mature), even those
who by reason of use have their senses
exercised to discern both good and evil.

They had the same problem then we face now
— that of growing. They were just like us. They
should have been teachers, but they still needed to
be taught. They couldn't be taught anything very
deep, but still had to be taught the milk. Paul said,
"I fed you on milk for you couldn't take the
meat."

The milk of the Word he's talking about here is
the preaching and staying with the first principles
of the doctrine of Christ (Hebrews 6:1-2). Paul
calls that the milk of the Word, not the strong
meat. When you still have to be taught the first
principles, you are still on the milk. It seems to me
that's about what we've done — and about what
we've had to do.

But how are we going to grow up? Look back at
this clause in Ephesians 4:13 which speaks about
growing in "the knowledge of the Son of God"
unto a perfect man.

Receiving the knowledge, feeding upon God's

Word: Until you gain a knowledge of the plan of God which He planned and sent the Lord Jesus to consummate...Until you gain a knowledge of what you are in Christ, and Christ in you...Until you gain a knowledge of what He did for you in His death, burial, resurrection, ascension, and seating at the right hand of the Father...Until you gain a knowledge of what He's doing for you right now, seated at the right hand of the Father where He ever liveth to make intercession for you...Until you gain a knowledge of your standing before the throne of God...Until you gain a knowledge of the fact that He defeated Satan and demons, and that all the forces of the rulers of the darkness of this world are dethroned powers, and that they can't rule over you.

When you do that, you're getting out beyond milk. But you can't preach that to some folks. You can't get too deep in there. To be honest with you, I know a lot of things I've never taught yet. Why not? Folks have to be ready for it. (Paul said in effect, "There are some things I'd like to teach you, but you couldn't bear it." They couldn't take it.) And I don't mean it's some farfetched revelation. It is the pure simple Word of God. But it is beyond where we have been. So we have to go slowly so folks can assimilate what we do give them.

The Wrong Diet

Why haven't we grown?

If we are real children of God, born of God, and we haven't grown, it is because we haven't had the right diet.

I don't blame people. I'm not scolding you. I'm thoroughly convinced the ministry is to blame. I believe most people — 99.99 out of 100 — would rise to the level of the Word of God for them if they knew it.

But just because a man is one of the ministry gifts — apostle, prophet, evangelist, pastor, teacher — doesn't mean he's a full grown Christian. It just means he has that calling on his life. He still has to develop and grow himself.

In the last church I pastored, during the winter of 1947 and 1948, I shut myself up in the church, sometimes for days at a time, with the Word. I would kneel and read the Bible on my knees. I read for hours, and for weeks. I had read it for years, of course, but this time I took those two prayers Paul prayed for the church at Ephesus — Ephesians 1:17-19, and 3:14-21.

I would leave one of my Bibles open to that place all week. And everytime I came into the building I would get on my knees and say, "Father, I'm praying these prayers for myself." If I had to make a call or something arose, when I'd

come back, even though I may have already done
it several times that day, I'd pray these prayers for
myself. "...That the eyes of my understanding be
enlightened, that I may know what is the hope of
His calling,...." And so on.

It didn't seem to do a bit of good for a while.
But I just kept on praying them. Then — after a
while — I began to get *revelation* from the Word.
(He couldn't have revealed the Word to me if I
hadn't been feeding on it.) It began to open up to
me!

Within a few weeks, 30 days or so, I'd learned
more than I'd learned in the previous 13 or 14
years of ministry put together. I said to my wife,
"What in the world have I been preaching? My,
my, my, that little old stuff I've been putting out
wasn't even milk. It was just bluejohn."

This didn't come just because I prayed. That
was just a part of it. I spent equal time, if not
more, with the Word as I did praying. You can't
build a prayer life just praying alone. It has to be
built upon God's Word.

So when the Bible speaks about our becoming a
perfect man, the terminology "knowledge of the
Son of God" is used (Ephesians 4:13). It infers that
it is this knowledge which will cause us to become
full grown, and cause us to become mature.

The Place of Right Teaching

We have failed to grow because of the lack of right teaching. God put teachers in the church. He set them in there. (Ephesians 4:11, I Corinthians 12:28.)

There are some ways all of us could do some teaching. From the natural standpoint we could tell some people what we know and could teach them to some extent. But on the other hand, there are those who are called of God, and anointed by the Spirit of God, to teach.

Of course, the Holy Ghost is also to be our teacher. But, after all, that is the Holy Ghost teaching us when He anoints men to teach. Some people get off on the idea that "No one can tell me anything. I don't need to be taught. I've got the Holy Ghost and I know as much as anyone knows." That is ignorance. God's Word declares that He set teachers in the Church to teach us.

I'm afraid though that much of our so-called teaching has been out of our minds and not out of our hearts. We've gained a general head knowledge, mental knowledge, of the Word but never got the spiritual import of it. Through the years what we've known as teaching has been so cold and dead and not much to it, we almost turn up our noses at the mention of it.

But the anointing of the Spirit of God upon genuine teaching of the Word of God is alive!

87

I didn't know the difference myself one day. I used to be a preacher. I could preach Spurgeon's sermons as well as anyone. I could read them and preach them word for word. I learned to sermonize and studied homiletics. I loved to preach with that old evangelistic fire and fervor. And, once in a while, I crack down on it and do it yet.

I was pastor of a church in North Central Texas in 1943. I'd never been a teacher until then. I didn't like to teach. It was their custom in this church that the pastor have at the Sunday School hour on Sunday morning the auditorium Bible class. It was made up of adult men and women. I didn't want to teach it. But it was their custom. I had a Sunday School book which I wouldn't look at all week. I studied the Bible and prepared sermons, but I wouldn't even look at this lesson until Saturday night. I knew I could read it over in 10 or 15 minutes and get up and tell it. They all seemed to enjoy it, but I was never so glad of anything in my life as when that class period was over. I wanted to preach.

But at 3 o'clock one Thursday afternoon in the parsonage of this church, God gave me a teaching gift. I knew it on the inside of me. I knew when it was born. I said out loud, "I can teach now."

To prove this, I started out in a most unlikely way. I didn't use any of the other main services where folks would come anyway. A ladies' prayer group met on Wednesday afternoons at the church and I started teaching them.

Do you know what surprised me? I could stand there just as still, and never move out of my tracks, never raise my hands, and the anointing would come on me greater than anything I ever sensed.

I began to teach those seven or eight ladies. They told their husbands and others. In two or three weeks, fifteen or twenty were coming. Some of the husbands took off from their jobs to come. Before you knew it, we had more people on Wednesday afternoon than on Wednesday night. Before you knew it, the church building was practically full.

That proved to me people want to learn and want to know.

Several years after I left that church I ran into one of those ladies. She said, "Thank God for those teaching sessions. That's all I've been living on for the past seven years. If I hadn't gotten that, I'm sure I would never have made it. I'm still feeding on it. I've never heard any teaching since then. All we get is preaching."

We need preaching all right. But believers need teaching. People of God need teaching.

Come back to Jesus and His ministry for a moment.

MATTHEW 9:35
35 And Jesus went about all the cities

and villages, teaching in their synagogues, and preaching the gospel of the
kingdom, and healing every sickness and
every disease among the people.

Reading through the four Gospels, everytime
He went into the synagogue, He always taught.

Down by the seashore one day He was teaching.
The crowd pushed Him back to the shore. A couple of fellows were there washing and mending
their nets as they had been fishing. One of them
was Simon Peter. Jesus asked if He could borrow
his boat, got in it and pushed a little way from
shore. And it says, "He sat down and taught the
people out of the ship" (Luke 5:3).

After he was baptized and the Holy Ghost came
upon Him in the bodily form as a dove, and He
was led by the Spirit into the wilderness and
tempted of the devil. And after He came back in
the power of the Spirit into Galilee, Luke 4:15
says, "And he taught in their synagogues, being
glorified of all."

These were the people of God of that day. The
synagogue would correspond to the church house
of today. Everytime He went into it, He taught.

The lack of right teaching is the primary reason
we've failed to grow. Certainly we can study for
ourselves and grow to some extent. But God also
put teachers in the Church to help us to grow, to
feed us upon God's Word.

90

The Fault of Inadequate Teaching

The Church has not majored in the things it should have. As one fellow said, "She has majored in the minors." When something was taught or preached, it was something of minor importance rather than something of major importance.

If you're going to grow, you'll have to be fed on the Word of God.

The Church has been strong in teaching man his need of righteousness, his weakness and inability to please God. It has been strong in denouncing sins in the believer. It has preached against unbelief, world conformity, and lack of faith.

But the Church has been sadly lacking in bringing forth the truth of what we are in Christ, and of how righteousness and faith are available.

A lot of people will tell you what you need, but they won't tell you how to get it. And you're not a bit better off. It's like one man said as they went away from church. His wife noticed something was wrong with him.

"What's the matter?" she said.

"I don't know," he said. "I'm disappointed and discouraged."

"With what?"

"With the church. With our pastor. He preached on faith this morning. He quoted all

91

those wonderful scriptures. 'All things are possible to him that believeth.' 'What things soever you desire, when you pray, believe that ye receive them, and you shall have them.' He told us what faith would do if we had it. And he told us we ought to get it. But he didn't tell us how. I'm just hanging out here in the air. I know I ought to get it. I know what it would do if I had it. But I don't know how to get it."

The real truth about it is he had faith all the time. Faith to be saved. If he had been taught correctly, he would have known he could have fed that measure of faith on God's Word and it would grow. He could use that same faith to receive healing for his body. He could use that same faith to get answers to prayer. He could use that same faith to be filled with the Holy Ghost. But he didn't know it.

You can't blame him, because what he heard hindered him more than it helped him. It didn't feed him. It took out of him.

There was a glow about the face of an obviously refined lady when she came up after the final service to shake hands with me. It was the first time she'd come up during the three-week meeting but I'd watched her blossom and open up.

She said, "Brother Hagin, thank you."

"For what?"

"For the Word. You've given me back my joy of salvation."

92

I said, "Praise the Lord."

She said, "I'm a visitor here. The last service I attended in my church, and I can understand that the pastor was trying to get us to pray; but instead of preaching it the right way to make us want to, he beat us over the head for nearly an hour. When he got through I went to the altar, got on my knees, and stuck my head under the altar. I said, 'Dear God, I don't know whether I'm saved or not. I don't know whether I have anything or not. I don't know where I am or who I am.' I stayed there and cried until about 1:30 in the afternoon. But you've encouraged us to pray. And I believe I'm praying more than I ever did in my life. I know I'm enjoying my fellowship with the Lord more than ever. I know I've got back the joy that I had when I was first a newborn babe."

One reason we haven't grown is we've preached to believers like they were sinners. We've treated them like they were sinners, and fed them like they were sinners, until we've undermined their faith.

We need to present God's blessings and God's power in such a way that folks want to do it, and get so hungry they can't help but do it. If you have to force people, it isn't going to work or be much of a blessing or benefit to them anyhow.

I'm talking about things that defeat us.

Our ministry, maybe unconsciously, has fed the congregations a psychology of unbelief. Instead of talking about what they have, they talk about what they don't have.

They talk about politics. Where did Jesus ever say to go into all the world and preach politics? He didn't. Where did you ever read that Jesus said, "Go into all the world and give a book review."? You didn't. He said, "Go into all the world and preach the Gospel."

Unconsciously, our ministry has fed us on a psychology of unbelief.

Most of the songs we sing are not really scriptural. (I'm talking about things that keep us from growing.) Most hymns put off redemption until after death.

> *"We don't have much here;*
> *Can't expect much here;*
> *But we're going to have it after*
> *awhile.*
> *We're going to have to do the best*
> *we can here;*
> *And wander around like a begger*
> *in this old gloomy world.*
> *When we all get to heaven, it'll be*
> *different."*

It would be different *now* if you'd believe God! Listen to the songs. Listen to the sermons.

They tell you we have the promise of eternal life — preaching to believers. We don't have the

94

promise of eternal life. The sinner does. We have it! Eternal life isn't something you're going to have when you get to heaven. It's something you have right now.

I JOHN 5:13
13 These things have I written unto you that believe on the name of the Son of God; that ye may know that ye have eternal life....

Present tense. "Have."

The Bible says that we *have* passed from death, spiritual death, unto life (I John 3:14). That Greek word for life here is "zoe." It's the same word that's used in John 3:16, "...that whosoever believeth in him should not perish, but have everlasting life."

Jesus said, "The thief cometh not, but for to steal, and to kill, and to destroy: I am come — (What did you come for, Jesus?) — I am come that they might have life..."

That's why He came! That we might have zoe! Life! Sometimes it's translated "life." Sometimes, "eternal life." And sometimes, "everlasting life." But it's all the same.

He said, "...I am come that they might have zoe, and that they might have it more abundantly" (John 10:10).

He said you can have this Life right now — and

95

you can have an abundance of it! That's why He came!

I listened to a radio preacher telling about how we have the promise of it, and we're going to have it one of these days. No, if you don't have it in this life, you'll never have it in the after life.

"For the wages of sin is death; but the gift of God is eternal life through Jesus Christ our Lord" (Romans 6:23). It's a gift you receive now! You receive this Life — this zoe, the life of God, the God-kind of Life — into your spirit, into your inward being.

It changes your life! This Life is the nature of God. It makes you a new creature and displaces that old nature you had on the inside of you. So you become a new man in Christ Jesus, with a new nature. "...old things are passed away; behold, all things are become new" (II Corinthians 5:17).

But most of our hymns we sing put redemption and eternal life off until after death. "We're going to have it then."

> "We're going to have rest when we
> get to heaven."

Do you know what the Bible teaches? It teaches we can have rest and peace right now. Jesus said:

MATTHEW 11:28-30
28 Come unto me, all ye that labour and are heavy laden, and I will give you rest.
29 Take my yoke upon you, and learn of

me; for I am meek and lowly in heart: and ye shall find rest unto your souls.
30 For my yoke is easy, and my burden is light.

The way some people talk, I just wonder what they're yoked up with. It's always a hard luck story. Always going through a trial. Always having a hard time. Always scraping the bottom of the barrel, or else under the barrel with the barrel on top. "Oh, this heavy burden we have to bear. We're going to lay down our heavy burdens one day."

Oh, no. You lay them down when you find Jesus. "My yoke is easy, and my burden is light," He said. It's not hard. It's not burdensome. It's not heavy.

What are they yoked up with? Unconsciously they've gotten yoked with unbelief. Though they actually belong to Jesus and have been born-again, they have gotten yoked up with unbelief and their burden became heavy instead of light. They couldn't sleep. Couldn't eat. They felt like they had butterflies in their stomach.

When there is rest in your soul, it will affect your body. It will affect your entire being.

> *"We're going to have victory after while."*

No, thank God, we have victory right now!

97

I JOHN 5:4

4   For whatsoever is born of God overcometh the world: and this is the victory
that overcometh the world, even our
faith.

> *"We're going to be overcomers
> when we get to heaven"*

No, we're overcomers now!
"If God be for us who can be against us?"
(Romans 8:31). He's on our side. We're victors
now. We're overcomers now.

> *"We're going to have peace with
> God when we get to heaven."*

That isn't what the Bible says. Romans 5:1 says,
"Therefore being justified by faith, we have peace
with God through our Lord Jesus Christ." It's
wonderful to have that peace.

The Bible does say, "There is no peace, saith the
Lord, unto the wicked" (Isaiah 48:22). If I didn't
have this peace I'd go to checking up on myself.
But He didn't say that to Christians. He said it to
sinners.

When you preach to Christians like they were
sinners you build that kind of consciousness in
them. You hold them under condemnation. They
can't grow. It's impossible. It's the wrong diet. It

98

isn't even the sincere milk of the Word.

Dr. John Alexander Dowie said, "Our songs are embalmed with unbelief." That's kept us from growing. We've sung those songs so much we think they're so. I don't want to bind you, but it would be better not to sing than to sing a bunch of junk, a bunch of unbelief.

> *"There will be no more failing when we get to heaven. We have nothing on this side and can't expect anything on this side except failure, misery, disappointment, and weakness."*

That isn't what the Word of God teaches. Paul said, "We're more than conquerors." Not just conquerors. More than conquerors!

"Yes, but Paul was an apostle," someone said.

Paul didn't say he was a conqueror because he was an apostle. He said, "...we are more than conquerors through him that loved us" (Romans 8:37). Christ didn't belong to Paul anymore than He does to us.

That doesn't mean you won't have any tests. That doesn't mean you won't have any trials. That doesn't mean it's just going to fall on you like ripe cherries off a tree. Or that you're going to float down the river of time on flowery beds of ease.

It didn't with Paul. He got in jail. He got his

back beat. He got his feet in stocks. He was in the innermost prison with every reason in the world to gripe and complain. But at midnight he and Silas prayed and sang praises to God!

When he got on board that ship a prisoner he said, "Sirs, I perceive that this voyage will be with hurt and much damage, not only of the lading and ship, but also of our lives" (Acts 27:10). They didn't pay any attention to him. Everything seemed to be all right. But before it was all over he was running the thing. He started on the bottom, but wound up captain of the boat.

Don't stay on the bottom! You don't have to. Do you know what brought Paul out? You can see it in his words.

When all hope that they should be saved was gone, old Paul stepped forth right in the midst of it with the answer. He'd heard from heaven. (We have God's Word and we've heard from heaven. It couldn't be anymore sure if an angel came down from heaven and wrote it with his finger in a granite rock. That couldn't be any more sure than God's written Word.)

Old Paul said, "Sirs . . . there stood by me this night the angel of God, whose I am, and whom I serve, Saying, Fear not, Paul; thou must be brought before Caesar: and, lo, God hath given thee all them that sail with thee. Wherefore, sirs, be of good cheer: for I believe God, that it shall be even as it was told me" (Acts 27:21-25).

I like that fellow Paul. He made three positive confessions: "I belong to God. I serve God. I believe God." And that's what caused him to rise.

If he'd been like most folks, he would have been whipped right in the midst of this crisis and he and the whole bunch would have gone down. For most folks would have said, "I've been trying to serve Him all these many years. The Lord knows I've been trying to serve Him. If He doesn't intervene somehow, we're all going."

And they would have gone. I'm not making fun. I'm just stating facts. That's what defeats us.

Paul didn't say, "I'm trying to serve Him." He said, "I am serving Him . . . The God whose I am . . . I belong to Him."

Someone said, "I hope I do."

Thank God, I know I do. I belong to Him. I serve Him. I believe Him.

PART IV

Chapter 8

WHAT MANNER OF MAN ARE YOU?

"Give none offence, neither to the Jews, nor to the Gentiles, nor to the church of God."
                    -I Corinthians 10:32

Here we have God's ethnic division of the human race: Jew, Gentile, Church of God. The Jew is ever a Jew. Gentile means the heathen world. Everyone outside of Christ who is not a Jew is a heathen, or a Gentile. The Church, the body of Christ, the new creation stands utterly alone.

Paul has another division in his writings: the natural man, the carnal man, and the spiritual man.

The natural man is one who has never yet passed out of death into life. He has never been born-again. He's never been recreated. He's never become a new creature in Christ Jesus.

The carnal man is a new creature. He has been born-again. But he's never developed or grown. It is sad but true that the carnal man may remain in this condition all his life long. He may never develop beyond the babyhood state of the new creation. He is governed by his body; by his physical senses, rather than by his spirit.

The spiritual man is one who has developed in divine things. His spirit has gained the ascendancy over his intellectual processes. And his spirit has gained the ascendancy over his body and his physical senses. God governs him through the Word.

Let's look carefully at these three men to see which one we are, and what we can do about it.

Chapter 9

THE NATURAL MAN

*"But the natural man receiveth not the things
of the Spirit of God: for they are foolishness
unto him: neither can he know them, because
they are spiritually discerned."*

-I Corinthians 2:14

Another translation says, "because they are
spiritually understood." If you understood the
things of God and spiritual things with your
mind, the natural man could understand them.
But you don't. You discern them, or understand
them, with your spirit.

The natural man is the unspiritual physical

105

man. His wisdom is earthly; earthly means
natural. James describes it:

JAMES 3:14-15
14 But if ye have bitter envying and
strife in your hearts, glory not, and lie
not against the truth.
15 This wisdom descendeth not from
above, but is earthly, sensual, devilish
(demonic).

The natural man is motivated by demons. He is
ruled by Satan. Oh no, I'm not saying he is demon
possessed. You see, all those who have never been
born-again have Satan as their god and father.
They are in the kingdom of darkness and they are
more or less ruled by Satan and demons. Remember Ephesians 6:12 says, "rulers of the darkness of
this world." So, the natural man is a Satan-ruled
man.

ROMANS 8:7-9
7 Because the carnal mind (other
translations call it "the mind of the
flesh") is enmity against God: for it is not
subject to the law of God, neither indeed
can be.
8 So then they that are in the flesh cannot please God. (This natural man cannot please God.)

9   But ye are not in the flesh, but in the Spirit, if so be that the Spirit of God dwell in you.

The natural man is the man that is motivated by the flesh; a physical man, not a spiritual man.

(I found out years ago it helped me in my studies in Romans, every place it says "flesh" to substitute the word "senses" or "physical senses." After all, the only way the flesh has any expression is through its physical senses. It will clear up a lot of thinking for you if you will do this.)

Knowledge Contrasted: Revelation — Natural Human

The natural man receives not the things of the Spirit of God for he cannot know them. You see, all the knowledge the natural man has is received through his five senses: sight, hearing, taste, smell, and touch. His mind is actually governed by his senses. I call this *natural human knowledge.* Others call it *sense knowledge.* That's a good term. The way it comes is through the five senses. Sense knowledge, natural human knowledge, is all that the natural man possesses.

But born-again believers have a knowledge that is above the flesh, above the senses. It could rightly be called *revelation knowledge.* This knowledge is revealed to us in the Word of God. It's above the

107

natural. The Bible brings you a revelation, or
reveals knowledge to you, which your physical
senses couldn't grasp. You couldn't understand it
even after revelation comes. But thank God, it's
there.

It is deeply important that every believer notice
the contrast between natural human knowledge,
or sense knowledge, and revelation knowledge.

Many modern theologians are not revelation
knowledge men, but sense knowledge men. It's all
in their minds. Most of the leaders of the church
world as a whole are actually sense knowledge
men. If they are saved, they are not spiritually
developed. Many aren't even saved, but just
natural men. They are governed by their physical
senses. That leads them to repudiate revelation
knowledge, or to give it second place in their lives.

The natural man cannot understand "the things
of the Spirit of God." They are foolishness to him.
The Bible is of the Spirit of God. It is not natural
human knowledge. Holy men of old wrote as they
were moved by the Spirit of God.

"Brother Hagin, this is refreshing," someone
said. "I am going to school and my professor said
concerning the Bible, 'If you can't understand it
and reason it out, forget it.' "

Can you understand and reason out God? Well
then, forget Him, according to this professor's (?)
advice. Can you understand and reason out with
your little peanut brain Jesus, the Son of God?

The virgin birth? (This professor had said, "The virgin birth is not reasonable. It didn't happen.") Can you understand and reason out the Holy Spirit? Can you understand and reason out divine healing? Can you understand and reason out the supernatural? No!

"Well then," he is saying, "if it doesn't make sense, forget it." This just proves what I am saying. He was motivated by the senses.

You can always locate these people. "Now common sense will tell you...." I know, but where did you ever read in the Bible that we walk by common sense? You didn't. It says that we walk by faith and not by sight (II Corinthians 5:7). It says, "...as many as are led by the Spirit of God, they are the sons of God" (Romans 8:14).

Natural man cannot understand the Bible because it is of the Spirit of God. It is in a realm he doesn't know anything about. Someone said, "What you're not up on, you're down on." The reason a lot of folks are down on a lot of things is, they're not up on them. If a man is a natural man and hasn't been born-again, he's not up on spiritual things. He doesn't know anything about them, so he is down on them.

The Natural Walk

EPHESIANS 2:1-3

1   And you hath he quickened, who were dead in trespasses and sins;
2   Wherein in time past ye walked according to the course of this world, according to the prince of the power of the air, the spirit that now worketh in the children of disobedience:
3   Among whom also we all had our conversation in times past in the lusts of our flesh, fulfilling the desires of the flesh and of the mind; and were by nature the children of wrath, even as others.

Here is a picture of the natural man walking. He is walking "according to the course of this world." He is walking according to the "prince of the power of the air." That's the devil. He is being ruled by the "spirit that now worketh in the children (sons) of disobedience." He is doing the "desires of the flesh" or of the senses. He is "by nature the child of wrath."

That's strong language. But it describes the man outside of Christ. Notice verses 11 and 12 of this same chapter.

110

EPHESIANS 2:11-12

11 Wherefore remember, that ye being in time past Gentiles in the flesh, who are called uncircumcision by that which is called the Circumcision in the flesh made by hands;

12 That at that time ye were without Christ, being aliens from the commonwealth of Israel, and strangers from the covenants of promise, having no hope, and without God in the world:

The American Revised Version of verse 12 reads, "that ye were at that time separate from Christ, alienated from the commonwealth of Israel, and strangers from the covenants of the promise, having no hope and without God in the world."

That was us before we were saved. And that's a picture of everybody who is not now saved. The Gentile has no more claim or hold on God today than he did then. As a Gentile he has no legal standing, no legal rights. But thank God, he can come and be born-again, and become a member of the body of Christ; then he has a standing and he has rights.

I CORINTHIANS 1:28

28 And base things of the world, and things which are despised, hath God

111

chosen, yea, and things which are not, to bring to nought things that are:

Here the Word of God is talking about us when He chose us in Christ. He calls us the "base things of the world." He calls us the "things which are despised." And, "things which are not."

The Centinary translation reveals the "things which are not" represented the slaves of the Roman Empire. They had no standing, no voice. They were just things, so to speak, which were not. But when they became Christians, they had a standing before God.

I Peter 2:10 says, "Which in time past were not a people, but are now the people of God:...." The Gentile has no standing. He is a "no people." With all his boasted culture, ability, and money, he has no voice; no standing with God. The picture of utter spiritual bondage, Ephesians 2:11 describes him as without hope, hopeless; and without God, Godless. *Hopeless* and *Godless.*

EPHESIANS 4:17-18
17 This I say therefore, and testify in the Lord, that ye henceforth walk not as other Gentiles walk, in the vanity of their mind,
18 Having the understanding darkened, being alienated from the life of God

112

through the ignorance that is in them,
because of the blindness of their heart:

They walk in the vanity of sense knowledge.
They walk in the vanity of their minds. They are
darkened in their understanding. They are alienated from the life of God. They are filled with
their own knowledge; ignorant of spiritual things.

Isn't that a picture of them?

But thank God there is a way. There's a way
out. There's a way to God. Jesus said, "I am the
way. I am the truth. I am the life."

Chapter 10

THE CARNAL MAN

> *"And I, brethren, could not speak unto you*
> *as unto spiritual, but as unto carnal, even as*
> *unto babes in Christ.*
> *I have fed you with milk, and not with*
> *meat: for hitherto ye were not able to bear it,*
> *neither yet now are ye able.*
> *For ye are yet carnal: for whereas there is*
> *among you envying, and strife, and divisions,*
> *are ye not carnal, and walk as men?"*
>   -I Corinthians 3:1-3

Who is this carnal man? He is the babe in
Christ. Not a newborn babe — when Paul wrote

these Corinthians they were not newborn people. He plainly infers they should have been beyond where they were in their spiritual development. They seem to have been in about the same boat as the Hebrew Christians (Hebrews 5:12).

Paul's letter to the Corinthians is written to born-again, Spirit-filled believers — even to a church which has all the gifts of the Spirit operating in it. He said to them, "ye come behind in no gift," bragging on them a little first before he started to correct them (I Corinthians 1:7). He specifically mentioned that they didn't come behind in utterance — that means the utterance gifts (I Corinthians 1:5). You can see that when you get over to where he began to correct them. They were all trying to talk in tongues at once.

Here is a thought that will help us in some of our thinking so we can grow. Spiritual gifts don't make you a full grown Christian. Often folks don't know what spirituality is. Some think being spiritual would be exercising a spiritual gift. That couldn't be so because here it plainly states these Corinthians were carnal and babes — and they had all the gifts of the Spirit operating in their church.

I've heard people say when a fellow Christian they thought to be carnal gave an utterance in tongues, or an interpretation, or prophecy, "That couldn't be the Lord."

I said, "Why?"

116

They'd say, "Well because they're carnal."

I said, "Do you mean to infer that carnal Christians can't have the Holy Ghost?"

"Yes."

"That can't be so because you have Him. And the church at Corinth had Him."

Can carnal Christians have the Holy Ghost? Certainly!

"Are carnal Christians saved?" someone asked this question to one of our Full Gospel magazines some years ago. I thought it was sort of cute the way it was answered: "Paul seemed to think so." Then they gave this scripture.

Actually the Greek word translated "carnal" has created much comment and no little confusion among Bible scholars. I think only in latter years has the Spirit of God made this word clear to us. In some scriptures it is translated "carnal" and in others it is translated "fleshly." It really means a man who is governed by his physical senses. That would be the flesh governing him. Though he is born-again and a new creature, he walks after the order of natural men.

Walks as a "Mere Man"

Listen again to what Paul wrote, "And I, brethren, could not speak unto you as unto spiritual (men), but as unto carnal (men), even as

117

unto babes in Christ...For ye are yet carnal: for whereas there is among you envying, and strife, and divisions, are ye not carnal, (NOW GET THIS) and walk as men?" Several modern translations read, "and walk as mere men?"

Paul talks about envy and some of the same things James did in talking about the natural man who had never been born-again. Paul is saying in effect, "Though you have been born-again, you are still walking as a mere man, as a common man, as the natural man who has never been born-again. You are walking just like the world men walk. There is envy and strife among them. You are letting your flesh dominate you."

One modern translation instead of saying "ye are carnal" says "you are body-ruled." That's a good translation. The outward man — the body which is not redeemed yet (thank God we will have a new body one day) — rules, instead of the inward man who is a new man in Christ and has the Holy Ghost dwelling in him dominating and ruling. Too much of the time in Christians the outward man dominates the inward. As long as he does, they will remain babies and carnal. They will walk just like world men — those outside of Christ — walk.

You'll run into these baby Christians who have never grown sometimes, and it is amazing to see how they think they are so spiritual yet they live in the flesh or in the senses.

I preached to a church once who before they received the baptism of the Holy Ghost and became Full Gospel were what we call old line holiness. Some of them almost thought it was a sin to take a bath. One did tell me it was a sin to use deodorant. Another one thought it was a sin to drink cokes.

It wasn't a little church. There were over 500 there the Sunday morning I preached and the Lord anointed me and gave me a message just for them. I never preached it afterwards. And although I was quite dignified then, much more than I am now, I jumped off the platform and ran up and down the aisles. I said, "People talk about worldliness. This is the most worldly church I ever preached in."

Man, they looked at me.

Then I began to tell them what worldliness and carnality is. I read what Paul had to say about the Corinthians, that there was envy and jealousy, debate, strife, and division. I said, "Personally, I thought Paul was writing a letter to this church, then I happened to look up there and it said Corinthians."

Some of them got so angry they were ready to fight. (That proved they were carnal, didn't it?) But it helped some of them.

Carnal Christians have not learned the love law nor the love walk. When you love one another you won't walk in envy and strife and jealousy and division. The Corinthians were born-again, filled with the Holy Ghost, they had gifts of the Spirit; yet they had not learned the love law, nor the love walk. When you are spiritual you learn that. When we begin walking in divine love, Christian love, Bible love, the God-kind of love, we stop being jealous; we stop strife and division and backbiting.

Backbiting, bitterness, and jealousy are signs of underdevelopment on the part of the believer. What causes these things? It's because people are selfish. As long as you are selfish, sensitive, and can be hurt, you are a babe in Christ and cannot grow.

Growing Out of Carnality

God wants us to grow. There is no other way to get out of the carnal state except to grow out of it. Peter said, "Desire the sincere milk of the Word that you may grow thereby." Paul said, "I have fed you with milk." Paul is trying to get these Corinthians to growing. He didn't tell them they weren't saved. That comes as a shock to some folks, but they'll just have to be shocked.

At the end of the chapter he said to them, "Therefore let no man glory in men. For all things are yours; Whether Paul, or Apollos, or Cephas, or the world, or life, or death, or things present, or things to come; all are yours; And ye are Christ's; and Christ is God's" (I Corinthians 3:21-23).

I am so glad for the Holy Spirit and for the Word of God. I am so glad the Lord has been patient with all of us and helps us.

I can remember praying away back in 1951 at the beginning of March down in the state of Alabama where I was holding a meeting. I was praying in tongues, in the spirit (I Corinthians 14:14).

(The devil and natural people — and sometimes even some carnal people — don't like this. But it'll help you, praise God. Most of what I know about the Bible, I learned by praying in tongues. What do I mean by that? The Spirit is to be your Teacher. If you will take enough time to pray in tongues, you'll get your mind and body quiet while your spirit is functioning. You are speaking out of your spirit. Then God can communicate with your spirit because it becomes sensitive to Him, for He is a Spirit.)

I prayed in tongues for almost 3 hours that day. Yet it seemed like only about 15 minutes. When I looked at my watch I couldn't believe it had gone by so fast. I had my eyes shut all that time praying.

During that time of praying the Lord took me through the first three chapters of I Corinthians — and it changed me. It changed the course of my ministry. It changed the course of my life. It made me a greater blessing to the Church. It enabled me

121

to do more than I'd ever done before. It helped me to do some growing.

He took me through the first chapter where Paul bragged on them a little and then began to tell them how they were babes and carnal.

He said to me, "If it had been you and some preachers you know writing to those people, you would have said, 'You backslidden buzzards need to pray through and get right with God.'"

That's probably exactly what I would have said up until then.

He said, "But Paul didn't call them buzzards. Paul didn't call them backslidden. He did call them carnal, and he did call them babes. When a baby cries, hitting him over the head isn't going to make him grow. Feeding him. Putting something into him, not taking something out of him, makes him grow. Don't take anything out of them. Put something into them.

"Do you remember J.W.?" He asked me.

I didn't.

"Do you remember Tuffy?" He said.

That was what we called him, Tuffy. Boy, that was putting it mildly. Tuffy wasn't a strong enough word for him. But even when He said that I still didn't remember because it had been so many years.

Then He called his whole name to me. And when He gave me his last name I said, "Oh yes, I remember."

The Lord refreshed my memory that day and it has enabled me to help others.

Tuffy's mother died when he was very young. His daddy was a motorman on the old interurban line from Waco to Denison, Texas and wasn't home much. So Tuffy was left to himself. He ran up and down the back alleys and got into the wrong crowd.

He was still in the 5th grade when I was, but he should have been in the 8th. And he was making a straight "D" report card — "D" was the lowest grade they gave in those days. He had been in trouble and I overheard the principal telling my Grandpa about it.

He asked, "What are we going to do with Tuffy? The judge called me again and he wants to send him to reform school. He's just been lenient on him because he knew he didn't have a mother."

I heard my Grandpa say, "Mr. Mac, if you'll do as I tell you, we'll make a man out of him. We'll make a useful citizen out of him."

The principal said, "Well, the judge is leaving it up to me for another thirty days."

Grandpa said, "Tell him to give us ninety days."

The principal agreed to call and ask for ninety days.

"Did you notice how he hangs around me?" Grandpa asked. "He's gotten to where he stays with me nearly all the time."

123

"Yes, I've noticed that," Mr. Mac said.

"It's because I'm the only one who puts anything into him. I tell him I've got confidence in him. I tell him I believe in him. Everybody else tells him he's no good. Everybody else tells him 'You're going to reform school.' Everybody else tells him he'll never make it. He's gotten where he won't even play on the playground anymore. He just hangs around with me. Now, in the first place, don't whip him anymore."

Mr. Mac would whip him one to three times a day, every single day. Sometimes folks do need whipping you understand, but other times it doesn't mean a thing in the world. You could hear the paddle all over that floor of the school, yet Tuffy would come back into the room laughing.

Grandpa told the principal, "I hid in the restroom in your office to watch and he's the one who stole the money out of your desk drawer."

They sold candy at lunch period and used the proceeds to buy playground equipment. Someone had stolen the money. Grandpa hid to see who got it. And it was Tuffy.

He said, "You have to start building confidence in him. So take him out of study periods and tell him, 'J.W., I need someone older than the rest to watch the office. Someone has been stealing the money.' Point right to where the money is and show him. If a dime is ever missing I'll put it back myself."

124

After they had this conversation at noon we went back to class. The first study period Mr. Mac came to the door and called Tuffy out. Everybody snickered. They knew he was going to get a whipping. They kept listening to hear that paddle. But he didn't come back. They wondered. But I knew exactly what was happening.

Mr. Mac had said to him. "Now J.W., you keep the office. We need someone older over here." He pulled the drawer open and showed him the money. "Here it is and someone has been stealing it." Of course, it was him.

The Lord reminded me how almost immediately I saw him begin to make passing grades. In fact, he did so well they began to move him up. He never went to reform school. He never went to the penitentiary. He grew up to be a useful citizen.

That day the Lord took me through the babyhood, childhood, and manhood stages of spiritual growth.

He told me, "Spiritual growth is like natural growth in a sense. Paul didn't just take out of these people. He corrected them gently all right, and showed them where they were missing it. But he didn't take everything away from them. He bragged about what they did have. And showed them there was more out there — encouraging them, 'Go to it! Get after it! It's your's!'

"Don't beat Christians over the head," He said.

125

Don't beat anyone over the head. Feed them. Find somewhere you can hook on with them. Don't fight other churches and other believers.

"Don't take anything away from anybody," He said. "Give them something. Put something into them."

That day changed my ministry. I started doing what the Lord said, and it worked.

Let's look again at what Paul said to them in the last part of that third chapter, "Therefore let no man glory in men. For all things are yours...."

Do you mean to tell me, Paul, that these baby Christians, these carnal Christians who were walking as mere men, that all things were theirs?

Yes. It all belonged to them. They may not have come to a knowledge of it yet, but it belonged to them. They may not have grown to a place where they could appreciate it and take advantage of it yet, but it belonged to them.

"...Whether Paul, or Apollos, or Cephas, or the world, or life, or death, or things present, or things to come; all are yours; (He didn't take anything from them. He said, 'It's all yours!') And ye are Christ's; and Christ is God's" (I Corinthians 3:21-23).

Chapter 11

THE SPIRITUAL MAN

"And I, brethren, could not speak unto you as unto spiritual...."

-I Corinthians 3:1

In other words Paul said, "I couldn't speak unto you as unto spiritual men." Isn't that a sad tragedy?

Who is this spiritual man? What are his characteristics?

EPHESIANS 1:3
3   Blessed be the God and Father of our
Lord Jesus Christ, who hath blessed us

with all spiritual blessings in heavenly
places in Christ:

The spiritual man is one who knows what
belongs to him in Christ Jesus, and takes advantage of it.

The spiritual man has drunk deeply at the foun-
tain. He has fed regularly at the table of the Lord.

The spiritual man has saturated himself in love,
the love of God.

Knowing the Father

This man has come to know the Father in reality.

There was a time in my life that I knew the
Lord Jesus, was filled with the Holy Ghost, had
preached a number of years, and had various gifts
of the Spirit operating at times in my life — but
somehow, on the inside of me, I knew that God
could become more real to me as my Father than a
father in the flesh. The Word said He was my
Father. And I knew in my spirit He could become
more real to me than my wife, more real to me
than either of my children. I knew in my heart —
and I said it out loud as I drove down the highway
on the way to revival meetings — that I knew
God could become more real to me than the automobile I drove. But — I knew He wasn't that

real to me.

It did not come overnight. It did not come in one month. It did not come in one year. But as I continued to do what the Bible said — to fellowship with the Father through the Word and through prayer — little by little, He became more and more real to me.

Until one day I was able to say, "He is more real to me and I know Him better than I know my wife. I'm more personally acquainted with God my Father than I am my wife. He is more real to me than my children. He is more real to me than the automobile I drive." (To be honest about it, not too many can say that, because natural things are more real to them than spiritual things.) I came to the place that every waking moment, even when I'd wake up in the nighttime, I'd be conscious of His presence — more conscious of His presence than I was of my wife's.

Knowing the Son

The spiritual man comes to know the Lord Jesus Christ in His great ministry at the right hand of God the Father. Every born-again believer knows the Lord Jesus Christ as Savior. But just being born-again will not cause you to grow. Just to know Him as Savior, you'll never be more than a baby. To grow, the believer must come to know

129

what he is in Christ, and what Christ is in him. He must come to know the present day ministry of the Lord Jesus Christ at the right hand of the Father.

Knowing the reality of Jesus' present day ministry did more for me in my spiritual growth than anything else. We need to grow up in knowing the reality of His ministry today as High Priest (Hebrews 4:14-16), as Advocate (I John 2:1), as Intercessor (Romans 8:34, Hebrews 7:25), as Shepherd (Psalm 23:1, John 10:14), as Lord!

Just because we've heard this taught is no sign we walk in the reality of it. It is as we feed upon it and become acquainted with the truth that we come into the full knowledge of the Son of God unto a perfect (mature) man.

Knowing the Holy Ghost

The spiritual man has come to know the blessed intimacy of the Holy Spirit as He is unveiled in the Word. You can be baptized with the Holy Ghost and speak in other tongues and never know this.

That's the sad thing about it. The baptism of the Holy Ghost has been preached in a way that isn't exactly right. And folks think that because "I have the baptism of the Holy Ghost" that's the end. But it isn't. It's just the beginning. And because of

130

wrong thinking they never really learn to know the Holy Spirit intimately and are cut off from growing.

As spiritual babes they received the infilling of the Holy Spirit and spoke with other tongues, and were all "taken up" with the outward manifestation. Certainly I believe in speaking in other tongues. Thank God for it. But you hear them talking about how "I felt," and they're trying to "feel" that way again.

(It doesn't make the least bit of difference to me if I ever "feel" that way again. I base nothing on feelings. I base everything on the Word.)

Then when they lose that "feeling" they thought they had, they think He's gone. But He isn't. Jesus said, "I will pray the Father, and he shall give you another Comforter, that he may abide with you for ever;" (John 14:16). He didn't say He would stay two weeks. He didn't say He would come on a vacation. He said the Holy Ghost would come "that he may abide with you forever."

Somebody said, "But Brother Hagin, don't you believe that if a man sins the Holy Ghost leaves him?"

Certainly not. If He ever left him he would be forever doomed and damned. He could never get back to God. The Holy Ghost doesn't go and come. Not a scripture in the Bible says so. David, after he'd had the woman's husband killed and

131

committed adultery with her, in his prayer of repentance said, "Take not thy holy spirit from me" (Psalm 51:11). Had the Holy Spirit left him, he could never get repentance. He could never pray. He could never come back.

And if He ever left you, that would be the end of it, too. He's still there to show you the way back to repentance. If you've sinned and failed He is still there—because He's a representative of God — to show you the way out and lead you back.

I've found that when I've missed God and sinned it isn't the Holy Ghost inside me who condemns me, it's my own spirit. Jesus said that He hadn't come into the world to condemn the world, but that the world through Him might be saved (John 3:17).

I found that the Holy Ghost was there to take the Word of God and open it up to me, to show me the ministry of Jesus for me today. Gently. Even when I'd missed it and was so ashamed of it I hated it with every fiber of my being, yet He was so sweet and so gentle to lead me, to show me the way out and the way back.

...as Indweller

I JOHN 4:4
4 Ye are of God, little children, and have overcome them: because greater is

he that is in you, than he that is in the world.

We need to become conscious of the Holy Spirit's indwelling presence, and learn to walk in the light of the Word on this subject. Then in time of crisis we would remain calm and collected because we'd know the Bible is so whether or not it "seems like" it is.

If you know "greater is he that is in me, than he that is in the world," when crisis comes, you won't have to run around like a chicken with his head cut off, flopping here and there trying to find help. You'll know Help is available. You'll know He is in there; the Greater One is in there. You're walking in intimate fellowship with Him, and He'll show you what to do.

In every crisis of life He shows me exactly what to do. On the inside of me, He'll rise up in me to give illumination to my mind, direction to my spirit. But He cannot do it if you're not sufficiently acquainted with Him to recognize it.

If you've been born-again and filled with the Holy Ghost, you have on the inside of you all you'll ever need to put you over. Jesus said, "I will pray the Father, and he shall give you another Comforter" (John 14:16). The Greek word translated Comforter also means — and the Amplified translation reads this way — Counselor, Helper, Intercessor, Advocate, Strengthener, and Standby.

133

What else would you ever need?

Get acquainted with the Holy Ghost through the Word. When you know what the Word says about Him, then you'll know what He'll do. You'll know how He will manifest Himself, and you'll know how to yield to Him. You'll know how to walk with Him. And you can grow spiritually.

...as Teacher

Here is an invitation, a precious invitation, a blessed invitation of the Spirit to go into the deep things of God:

> I CORINTHIANS 2:12
> 12 Now we have received, not the spirit of the world, but the spirit which is of God; that we might know the things that are freely given to us of God.

We didn't receive the spirit of the world — we received the Holy Spirit, the Spirit which is of God. Why? For what purpose? *That we might know something.*

Jesus said of Him, "He will teach you. He will guide you into all truth. He will show you things to come. He will receive of mine and show it unto you."

134

The "things that are freely given to us" are the things Paul's talking about in Ephesians 1:3, "all spiritual blessings in heavenly places in Christ." And they are the things:

I CORINTHIANS 2:13
13 Which things also we speak, not in the words which man's wisdom teacheth, but which the Holy Ghost teacheth; comparing spiritual things with spiritual.

Now notice something Paul said earlier in this chapter, "Howbeit we speak wisdom among them that are perfect (mature — baby Christians wouldn't get it): yet not the wisdom of this world, *nor of the princes of this world, that come to nought:"* (verse 13). Another translation reads, *"nor of the dethroned powers of this world."* That's involved in the all things He has done for us.

Jesus — in His death, burial, and resurrection — dethroned the devil and all the spiritual forces that had ruled this earth from the time Adam sold out to him in the garden. Adam was the god of this world. God gave him dominion over all the work of His hand. But Adam committed high treason and sold out to the devil. Then the devil became the god of this world (II Corinthians 4:4).

Ephesians 6:12 says, 'For we wrestle not against flesh and blood, but against principalities, against powers, against the rulers of the darkness of this

135

world, against spiritual wickedness in high places."

Jesus dethroned them! In His great plan of redemption which God planned and sent Jesus to consummate, these powers are dethroned. They can't rule over us any more, but we can rule over them in the name of Jesus.

Now — this wisdom is "not in the words which man's wisdom teacheth, but which the Holy Ghost teacheth;" (I Corinthians 2:13). It is an unveiling of spiritual things. You couldn't have knowledge from the natural, to save your life, that Jesus defeated the devil. You couldn't see Him do it. The disciples saw Him dying at Calvary, but they didn't know why He died. He was with them and had tried to tell them. But they didn't know why He died when He died. After He appeared to them they said, "Lord wilt thou at this time restore again the kingdom to Israel?" It wasn't until the Holy Ghost came and began to teach them, that they understood the plan of salvation and what God did for them in redemption. This couldn't be seen with the natural eye. The natural man couldn't understand it at all. It is an unveiling of spiritual things by the aid and the energy of the Spirit of God Himself.

His Inheritance

The spiritual man knows his inheritance.

COLOSSIANS 1:12-14
12 Giving thanks unto the Father,
which hath made us meet to be partakers
of the inheritance of the saints in light:
13 Who hath delivered us from the
power of darkness, and hath translated us
into the kingdom of his dear Son:
14 In whom we have redemption
through his blood, even the forgiveness
of sins:

Another translation reads, "Giving thanks unto the Father, who has given us the ability...." If He "made us meet," He gave us the ability. To do what? To enjoy our share of the inheritance of the saints in light!

The spiritual man will know what his inheritance is in the light — for the light of God's Word will shine in and open it to him. He'll know he has the Ability to enjoy it.

His Ability

For God has given us our Ability. He is our Ability. That Ability reveals itself in unveiling the treasures of the grace of God that belong to us.

Our thinking has been so shallow in some areas we have been robbed of God's blessings. For instance, we have quoted Acts 1:8, "But ye shall receive power, after that the Holy Ghost is come upon you: and ye shall be witnesses unto me both in Jerusalem, and in all Judaea, and in Samaria, and unto the uttermost part of the earth," and without studying it any we've put emphasis on the word "power" not realizing what the word "power" means here.

I was pastor of a community church when I received the baptism of the Holy Ghost and spoke with other tongues. To hear Full Gospel people talk about this "power" I thought it would be some kind of a great overwhelming physical and emotional experience. But all I did was talk in tongues. (Yet when I read down through the Acts of the Apostles that was all I could find they did. So if the other would have been important, the Bible would have said something about it.) And though I talked in tongues for an hour and a half and sang three songs in tongues — as I talked in tongues I said in my mind, "My, my, my, I've had a greater blessing than this many times just out praying by myself."

But, you see, receiving the Holy Ghost isn't getting a blessing. You can get blessings beforehand and you can get blessings afterwards. It is receiving a Divine Personality to come into you and

138

dwell in your spirit!

I didn't know that. I'd shake myself, and feel myself, and think, "My, my, my, I don't have any more power now than I ever had."

So I went back to my church and never said a word about it. I didn't seem to have any more power to preach, but the congregation began to tell it.

They said, "You have something you didn't have."

I said, "What is it?"

"Well, it's a greater ability than you had. It's a greater punch."

I looked up this word "power" from Acts 1:8 in Young's Concordance. And I found out that this Greek word translated "power" here also means "ability."

My congregation could see I had more ability to preach than I did have. I had my mind hung up on the "power." God said that we would receive an ability. An ability to witness. We've overlooked the ability trying to find the power.

John called it an unction, he called it an anointing, he said it is in you. When you know the Ability of God is in there then you know what he meant when he said, "Greater is he that is in you."

When you know this, then when you hit that hard place, you can just lean back on Him instead of fighting and trying to pray the power down or work it up. You can just lean back and laugh. You can shout all the way through because you know the Greater One is in there. He'll put you over. He'll make you a success. He'll bring you out.

The spiritual man is going to come to know this, but the baby doesn't know this. The baby knows he has had an experience.

God has made us meet, He has given us the Ability. That ability comes with the infilling of the Holy Ghost. Yes, the ability to witness. But it doesn't stop there. He has given us the ability to enjoy our inheritance.

Deliverance, redemption, is our inheritance (Colossians 1:13-14). We have been delivered out of Satan's authority. Satan has no authority over you, or over me, or over the Church. Let's don't let him take any. We have been delivered out of his power or authority and translated into the kingdom of His dear Son (verse 13).

Governed by the Word

You're in the place of His protection and His care. You're in the place where you feed upon the bread of heaven. The Word of God is the bread. Jesus said, "Man shall not live by bread alone, but by every word that proceedeth out of the mouth of God." The manna of heaven is the Word of God. As you feed on this Word, you will grow up spiritually into the image and unto the stature of the Son of God.

And that's the only way you'll ever get there. As important as prayer is, you won't get there by praying. Though fasting may have a place, you won't get there by fasting. Though self-denial may have a place in the Christian life, you won't get there by self-denial. Though experience has a place in the Christian life — and thank God for experiences — but though you may have had many wonderful experiences or many wonderful visions or revelations, they will not get you there. Nor will spiritual gifts get you there. These things have their place and their purpose, but the Bible tells you exactly how to get there. It comes by the knowledge of the Word.

The spiritual man is the one in whom the Word has gained the ascendancy over his mind and over his body. It has brought him into harmony with the will of God, for the Word of God is the will of God.

PART V

Chapter 12

THE RIGHT DIET

You have to have the right diet if you're going to grow.

What is it?

Well, of course, the entire Word of God. But particularly the New Testament. Because we live under the New Covenant, not under the Old Covenant. Some things said back there don't apply to us. Many principles do, but other things don't. They apply to the Jews.

Certain sections of the New Testament are written especially for your benefit. (Other sections, like the four Gospels, are for the benefit of not just Christians and believers, but the world and sinners.) There are Letters which are written directly to the Church. Spend most of your time feeding on the Epistles.

No one told me to do it, but I believe that on the bed of affliction where I was born-again as a boy of 15, I unconsciously yielded and was led by the Spirit of God. The first time I was physically able to have a Bible brought to my bed, when I looked at it and saw it said "Old Testament" and "New Testament" I reasoned that the New must take the place of the Old. So I started in with Matthew.

I eventually saw that the Letters were written to the Church — from Paul's writings to the Romans and the Corinthians right on down through the Letters of Peter and John. Through these many years I've spent 90% of my study of the Word of God here. It's the diet I'm supposed to have. It's the message that was written to me. There are things there which can't be found any place else. Paul plainly stated about the mystery of this revelation that it was "now" made manifest (Romans 16:25-26).

Let your diet be mainly made up of the Epistles or Letters which were written to the Church. Particularly let it consist of I Corinthians 13 and the First Epistle of John.

Get an Amplified translation of I Corinthians 13 and go over it carefully. It will do just what its name implies — it will amplify those verses and

144

help you understand them even better.

Feed on all five chapters of I John.

You will find that in these two writings — I Corinthians 13 and I John — the great love teachings are unveiled and revealed. John comes back to it again and again:

"We know that we have passed from death unto life, because we love the brethren" (I John 3:14).

"But whoso hath this world's good, and seeth his brother have need, and shutteth up his bowels of compassion from him, how dwelleth the love of God in him?" (I John 3:17).

"But whoso keepeth his word, in him verily is the love of God perfected:...." (I John 2:5).

"There is no fear in love; but perfect love casteth out fear...He that feareth is not made perfect in love" (I John 4:18).

These are just a few of the many such statements there.

God's nature is Love. As His child you have the Love nature in you. Yet that nature has to be fed in order for it to grow. Unless you feed where this is found it will not grow and develop in your life.

I am thoroughly convinced that if every Christian would get into I Corinthians 13 and I John and live there awhile, it would only be a little while until they'd be so different they'd have to pinch themselves and say, "Is this me?"

It wouldn't be long until their homes would be so different it would be absolutely amazing. For

145

one statement in I Corinthians 13 is, "(Love) seeketh not her own" (verse 5). The babes are always seeking their own — naturally and spiritually, too. The baby is always saying, "Mother, Johnny has my cart." Or, "Mary has my doll." Strife. Quarreling over their own. The quarrels in our homes, the divorces, give us a picture of the babyhood state of the modern church. Those who walk in love and have matured in love wouldn't be acting this way. This babyhood condition in the church can be remedied only by the study, the feeding upon, and the putting into practice of the Word of God.

Study the plan of redemption. Find out what you are in Christ — and what Christ is in you. Find out your standing before God. Find out that you are the righteousness of God in Christ Jesus. Find out what He did for you in His death, burial, resurrection, ascension, and seating at the right hand of the Father. Find out what He is doing for you right now at the right hand of the Father in His present day ministry where He ever liveth to make intercession for us. This knowledge will help you grow out of the babyhood state into a fullgrown man in Christ.

Here's God's commentary on the subject:

I CORINTHIANS 4:7
7 For who maketh thee to differ from another? and what hast thou that thou

146

didst not receive? now if thou didst receive it, why dost thou glory, as if thou hadst not received it?

Whatever we have from God we received by grace.

EPHESIANS 4:7
7 But unto every one of us is given grace according to the measure of the gift of Christ.

Each believer — though born-again as a babe — has a measure, a deposit of grace that will meet every emergency in his life.

Every believer has the same new birth, the same Eternal Life, the same Love of God, the same grace, the same Holy Spirit (we know Him first in a measure in the new birth, but then there is the fullness of the Spirit available to us), the same Eternal Intercessor, Jesus Christ, the same matchless Heavenly Father.

If all this be true, then there is no reason for us to be weak and to remain babies when by reason of time we should be developed.

Let's look again at the full grown believer in Ephesians 4:13-14, "Till we all come in the unity of the faith, and of the knowledge of the Son of God, unto a perfect man, unto the measure of the stature of the fulness of Christ: That we hence-

147

forth be no more children...."

God never planned on your remaining a baby spiritually any more than He planned on your remaining a baby physically, or mentally.

We're attracted to little babies. They're so sweet and wonderful. But wouldn't it be sad for a little one to live twenty or twenty-five years and not grow physically or mentally? I saw an individual like that — thirty-eight years old and still in a bassinet. His mother nearing seventy would pin a diaper on him and feed him just as you would a small baby. How your heart bleeds for them. Aged parents, the other children grown and married, and they are left with this one.

But, you know, how sad it is for Christians. Many are in the same boat. If we could see spiritually, they've never developed. They're still babies. Forty years old and still a baby. Selfish. Sensitive. Easily hurt. Envious. Jealous.

A deacon, an older man who'd been saved and filled with the Holy Ghost thirty years came crying to the parsonage bawling like a baby, "Brother Hagin, you don't visit me like you do some of the others. I saw your car three times last week over at Brother So-and-so's house."

I said, "Yes, and there's another verse right under that. I'm not coming to see you either. You get up and testify, 'I was saved thirty years ago last October, filled with the Holy Ghost for thirty years.' "A big thirty year old baby.

This man he'd seen me visiting had just gotten saved in our meeting a week or so before. Because he was just a newborn baby he'd stumbled around and missed it. God talked to me in my heart and sent me out there to deal with him. So I went out to help him.

I said to this deacon, "You don't need anyone running out there to visit you and feed you the bottle. You need to be out visiting others yourself."

We have churches full of babies. Take their bottles away and you have a cry on your hands. Try to get them to get up and get out of the spiritual nursery and give up their bed to some newborn babe and they wouldn't do it for anything in the world.

Another deacon, a leader, supposed to be setting an example in the church, got mad and wouldn't come. I knew something happened because his wife kept coming. (Some men would be in a mess if they didn't have good wives.) I saw him in town and he would hardly talk to me. He was hard and cold, puffed up like a toad frog.

His wife was a sweet person and I asked her, "What's wrong with him?"

She said, "Oh, he's mad about something. He went home from church and went to bed. He wouldn't even talk to me for three days. I finally just asked him what was wrong. I thought maybe it was me. But it wasn't. And it's not exactly you. Somebody sat in his pew. He always sits right here in the second pew, the second seat from the end. When he got here and someone was sitting there, he got so mad he stood up. He wouldn't sit anywhere else."

A man like that isn't fit to be a deacon.

God never planned that he would remain a spiritual baby. He wants us to grow spiritually.

Exhortations to Growth and Spirituality

EPHESIANS 3:20
20 Now unto him that is able to do exceeding abundantly above all that we ask or think, according to the power that worketh in us.

There is no need for us to stay in a state of babyhood, or underdevelopment. We have the Power of God working in us! We have the Ability of God working in us! But instead of yielding to that, babies yield to the flesh.

PHILIPPIANS 4:13
13 I can do all things through Christ which strengtheneth me.

See! No place for underdevelopment!

150

HEBREWS 5:11

11 Of whom we have many things to say, and hard to be uttered, seeing ye are dull of hearing.

The Book of Hebrews isn't written to the world; it's written to Christians, to believers. If the believer isn't careful, he can become dull of hearing so that the Word cannot reach him. This can hold him in that babyhood state and carnality. Going on with the next verse...

HEBREWS 5:12

12 For when for the time ye ought to be teachers, ye have need that one teach you again which be the first principles of the oracles of God; and are become such as have need of milk, and not of strong meat.

This doesn't mean that everyone of them would have a teaching gift. It means that because they have known and have been fed on the Word themselves, they ought to be able to teach someone else. Every believer ought to aspire to be the teacher of at least one. But you can't teach if you're a babe, and still on milk.

HEBREWS 5:13-14

13 For every one that useth milk is

unskilful in the word of righteousness:
for he is a babe. But strong meat
belongeth to them that are of full age,....

Paul talks about the same things in Timothy.

II TIMOTHY 3:7
7   Ever learning, and never able to come
to the knowledge of the truth.

Isn't that the picture of some today? Going to
church Sunday after Sunday, ever learning, yet
never arriving. If calamity comes, if sickness
comes, if the loss of property, or the death of loved
ones comes, they stand paralyzed and helpless in
the presence of the enemy.

They have the resources of God because they
are believers and He has made provision for them.
They have the Ability of God. They have His loving Words. But they have never taken advantage
of it. They never avail themselves of the riches
that are theirs when the crises come.

Crises of life come to all of us. But it makes a big
difference when a crisis comes whether you are in
the carnality babyhood stage, or whether you have
grown at least to some extent.

Children who have never developed when crisis
comes, are unable to take advantage of what
belongs to them. They've stayed in their infancy.
My what a picture.

152

Ephesians 5:1 and 2 shows what they could be.

EPHESIANS 5:1-2
1 Be ye therefore followers of God, as dear children;
2 And walk in love, as Christ also hath loved us, and hath given himself for us an offering and a sacrifice to God for a sweet-smelling savour.

I like another translation which reads, "Be ye therefore imitators of God, as beloved children." What's it talking about to follow God? to imitate God?

Remember, God is Love. In the First Epistle of John, which I wanted you to stay in for awhile, John says in effect that if you walk in love, then you walk in God, and God is in you and you're in God, because God is love.

Imitate God in love. "God so loved the world." He loved us while we were yet sinners. Well, imitate Him in that. It's easy to love those who love you. Anybody can do that. But we're supposed to do like God — to imitate Him in love — and love the unlovely, love the unlovable, love our enemies.

You can't do that unless you have the Love of God in you. And you'll not do it unless you grow in Love.

When you're sensitive and easily hurt, it doesn't

153

take enemies outside the body of Christ, but just a
believer, a brother in the Lord, to do something
that doesn't amount to a hill of beans and you're
so easily hurt you're almost ready to cut his head
off.

Be imitators of God walking in Love. This is our
privilege. This is where we should and could live.
We have this New Covenant law to govern us as a
Church:

> JOHN 13:34-35
> 34 A new commandment I give unto
> you, That ye love one another; as I have
> loved you, that ye also love one another.
> 35 By this shall all men know that ye are
> my disciples, if ye have love one to
> another.

Fruit of the Human Spirit

Love is the first fruit of the human spirit when
you are born-again. It's not the fruit of the Holy
Spirit. The translators were entirely wrong in putting a capital "S" in Galatians 5:22. It refers to the
human spirit.

Jesus said, "I am the vine, ye are the branches"
(John 15:5).

Where does the fruit grow?

On the branches.

154

Who are the branches? The Holy Spirit?

No. We are.

This fruit of the spirit (Galatians 5:22) is fruit that grows in your life because of the Life of Christ within.

How are you going to know and tell that you are saved?

"We know that we have passed from death unto life, because we love the brethren" (I John 3:14).

This is the fruit of the recreated, born-again human spirit (Galatians 5:22-23). You can take each fruit of the spirit and prove by the Bible that if you're saved you have it. For instance, one is peace. Romans 5:1 says, "Therefore being justified by faith, we have peace with God through our Lord Jesus Christ."

If you are born-again, this Love is in you. You may not be practicing it. But it's in your inward man, your spirit.

If you're ever going to grow and develop out of the babyhood state, you will have to learn to feed this Love nature on the Word of God, and exercise this love nature in the arena of life. Then you will grow in Love.

You'll not do it any other way. You could sit around all day and pray, "God, give me love. God, help me love my brother. God, help me love the world," and it wouldn't do any more good than to twiddle your thumbs and say, "Twinkle, twinkle, little star; How I wonder what you are."

But when you recognize the Bible teaches that because you are born of God you are born of Love; that you are made a partaker of the divine nature, God's nature, which is Love; and you have it, a measure of it at least...and then you get ready to feed that love nature on the Word of God, and to put it into practice...you will begin spiritual development and growth. And not until.

Love is absolutely to govern the heart life of the Church.

I CORINTHIANS 10:24
24 Let no man seek his own, but every man another's wealth (or good).

How many of us are seeking our own good? Most of us. When love does not rule, then the motives of life become distorted; conduct becomes abnormal, and the body rules the spirit causing the mind to be brought into captivity to earthly things.

Renewing the Mind

ROMANS 12:2
2   And be not conformed to this world: but be ye transformed by the renewing of your mind, that ye may prove what is that good, and acceptable, and perfect, will of God.

156

The primal need of man is to have his mind renewed.

"And be not conformed to this world...." (Another translation says, "Be not conformed to this age.") Don't think like this age thinks! Don't think like this generation thinks. Don't think like this world thinks! Don't be fashioned according to this world, or this age.

"...but be ye transformed by the renewing of your mind, that ye may prove what is that good, and acceptable, and perfect, will of God." This infers that if your mind is renewed — and it becomes renewed by the Word of God — then you will know what is the good, the acceptable (one translation says "permissive"), and the perfect will of God. But until your mind is renewed, you will stay in the state of babyhood.

COLOSSIANS 3:10
10 And have put on the new man, which is renewed in knowledge after the image of him that created him:

It is deeply important that the believer's mind be renewed after the image of Jesus. That's one reason He sent the Holy Ghost to indwell us and be our Teacher and Guide. He said, "Howbeit when he, the Spirit of truth, is come, he will guide you into all truth:..." (This can only come as the

157

Spirit, through the Word, guides us into the reality of our redemption in Christ.) "...for he shall not speak of himself; but whatsoever he shall hear, that shall he speak: and he will shew you things to come" (John 16:13).

> EPHESIANS 4:23-24
> 23 And be renewed in the spirit of your mind;
> 24 And that ye put on the new man, which after God is created in righteousness and true holiness.

You know as well as I, that if you put on the new man created after God in righteousness and true holiness, that is going to be the end of envyings, jealousies, strifes, and divisions, isn't it? Therefore, you wouldn't be a babe in that carnal state anymore.

> ROMANS 12:1-2
> 1 I beseech you therefore, brethren, by the mercies of God, that ye present your bodies a living sacrifice, holy, acceptable unto God, which is your reasonable service.
> 2 And be not conformed to this world: but be ye transformed by the renewing of your mind....

158

Paul didn't write this to unsaved people. It came as a real shock to me, after fifteen years in the ministry, when I realized that Paul is saying to people who are born-again and filled with the Holy Ghost that it hadn't affected their bodies or their minds.

Therefore the new birth and the baptism of the Holy Spirit are not mental experiences, nor physical experiences, but spiritual experiences.

After you are born-again, and after you are filled with the Holy Ghost, it is up to you to do something with your body. It is up to you to do something with your mind.

The real you is the man on the inside — the spirit man. You are to present your body to God. (He does want transfigured bodies.) And you are to get your mind renewed. How? With the Word of God. By meditating on and practicing the Word of God.

Chapter 13

A WORD OF ENCOURAGEMENT

Don't become discouraged because you don't become a full grown Christian overnight. You didn't become a full grown human overnight.

The Bible says for us to examine ourselves. It doesn't say for me to examine you, or for you to examine me. But to examine yourself. As I examine myself, in some areas I think I'm growing pretty well, that I'm pretty well matured. But as I look at another place, it seems like I'm still a baby in that area. And then as I look in another area it seems like I'm in the childhood state. I dare say you are in the same boat.

Is anyone fully grown up? fully spiritual?

already perfected in love? I don't think so. But, praise God, we're on our way!

Don't be discouraged because you don't get there overnight. You didn't become discouraged because you went one week to school and they didn't graduate you the next. No, you stayed on in the first grade and were tickled to get in the second grade the next year.

You will not grow up spiritually overnight any more than you grew up mentally or physically overnight. But there's one thing about it — there's no need of your not growing.

It is always the greatest concern of my life whether or not I know more about God and have grown any this year above last year.

I believe in going on to perfection. I'm not perfect yet, are you? But I'm going on. I'm not going to stop and quit just because I didn't grow up last week, or because I made a mistake or failed.

The full grown Christian won't do that either, because he knows that Jesus is right there to represent him at the right hand of the Father.

Every step out of love is sin. Too often we've gotten in our minds that you didn't sin unless you broke one of the ten commandments. But that was the law of the Old Covenant. The new law of the New Covenant is that we love one another. So every word said out of love is sin. Every act made out of love is sin.

But this Epistle written to the Church says, "My

little children, these things write I unto you, that ye sin not. And if any man sin, we have an advocate with the Father, Jesus Christ the righteous" (I John 2:1).

As I look back — and I guess anyone who has had any spiritual growth is the same way, we thought we were doing pretty well spiritually, back when we were in some areas of babyhood. We thought we were living practically sinless. We met all the human standards they set for us, so we thought we were practically sinless. But then, as we grow up a little and develop spiritually, and we look back we see we were sinning more than we thought we were. We come to find out we missed it more than we thought we did. We failed to walk in love.

But just because we failed, we didn't stay there. We got up and went again.

It is the knowledge of God's Word that helps us to grow. That Word is spiritual food — food for our spirits!

ABOUT THE AUTHOR

The ministry of Kenneth E. Hagin has spanned more than 60 years since God miraculously healed him of a deformed heart and incurable blood disease at the age of 17. Today the scope of Kenneth Hagin Ministries is worldwide. The ministry's radio program, "Faith Seminar of the Air," is heard coast to coast in the U. S. and reaches more than 100 nations. Other outreaches include: *The Word of Faith*, a free monthly magazine; crusades, conducted nationwide; RHEMA Correspondence Bible School; RHEMA Bible Training Center; RHEMA Alumni Association and RHEMA Ministerial Association International; and a prison ministry.

RHEMA
Bible Training Cente

Want to reach the height of your potential?

RHEMA can ta you the

I proven instructors
I alumni benefits
I career placement
I hands-on experience
I curriculum you can use

Do you desire —
- to find and effectively fulfill God's plan for your life?
- to know how to "rightly divide the Word of truth"?
- to learn how to follow and flow with the Spirit of God?
- to run your God-given race with excellence and integrity
- to become not only a laborer but a *skilled* laborer?

If so, then RHEMA Bible Training Center is here for you!

For a free video and full-color catalog, call:
1-888-28-FAITH — Offer #863
(1-888-283-2484)
www.rhema.org

RHEMA Bible Training Center admits students of any race, color, or ethnic origin.

The Word of Faith

The Word of Faith is a full-color magazine with faith-building teaching articles by Rev. Kenneth E. Hagin and Rev. Kenneth Hagin Jr.

The Word of Faith also includes encouraging true-life stories of Christians overcoming circumstances through God's Word, and information on the various outreaches of Kenneth Hagin Ministries and RHEMA Bible Church.

To receive a free subscription to *The Word of Faith*, call:

1-888-28-FAITH — Offer #864

(1-888-283-2484)

www.rhema.org

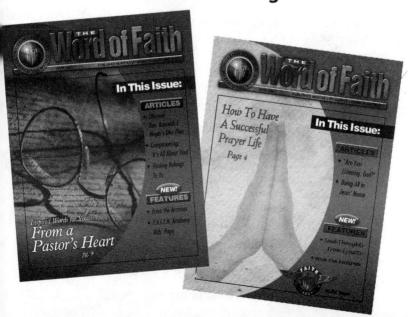

RHEMA

Correspondence Bible School

• Flexible •

Enroll anytime: choose your topic of study; study at your own pace!

• Affordable •

Pay as you go — only $25 per lesson!

(Price subject to change without notice.)

• Profitable •

"Words cannot adequately describe the tremendous impact RCBS h. had on my life. I have learned so much, and I am always sharing n newfound knowledge with everyone I can. I feel like a blind person wl has just had his eyes opened!"

Louisia.

"RCBS has been a stepping-stone in my growing faith to serve God wi the authority that He has given the Church over all the power of t enemy!"

New Yo

The RHEMA Correspondence Bible School is a home Bible stu course that can help you in your everyday life!

This course of study has been designed with the layman in mind, w practical teaching on prayer, faith, healing, Spirit-led living, and m more to help you live a victorious Christian life!

For enrollment information and course listing call today!
1-888-28-FAITH — Offer #862
(1-888-283-2484)
www.rhema.org